the rest is

SARA & SAM HARGREAVES

The Rest Is Worship
Copyright © 2023 Sara & Sam Hargreaves

Published by Music and Worship Foundation CIO (MWF).
Registered office: 8a Horley Close, Bexleyheath, Kent, DA6 7HS.
www.mwf.org.uk
MWF is a registered charity, number 1175280.

ISBN 978-1-8382312-9-3.
A catalogue record for this book is available from the British Library.

Illustrations and cover design by Gemma Scharnowski.

With thanks to Gemma & Timo Scharnowski for extensive input, Ron Jones for proofreading and our MWF trustees for believing in this project. Also much appreciation to those who preordered and financially supported this project in our November 2022 giving campaign.

Engage Worship is a ministry of the Music and Worship Foundation CIO. We exist to resource and train local churches for creative, sustainable and world-changing worship. For free downloadable resources, information on our training events or to order further books visit **engageworship.org**

Contents

Part One:

the invitation to rest

Chapter 1
Messed Up Boxes

As humans, we love putting things in boxes. Organising things so that they are neat and distinct. Our box marked "rest" might contain: a lie-in, watching TV, reading a trashy novel, having some time off... those kinds of things. Meanwhile our box marked "worship" may hold: singing, church services, prayer, liturgy... religious or "spiritual" sounding things.

In the last few years, we - Sara and Sam - have found God messing up our boxes. Sometimes it feels as if God is like a toddler who has got into the cereal cupboard. Suddenly the Cheerios, granola and Weetabix are all on the floor mixed together. It's hard to tell where one ends and the other begins.

Rest and worship are not exactly the same things, but the areas of overlap are far bigger than we had ever imagined. Rather than starting with a logical explanation of what we mean, we're going to try and paint three word pictures that might help you experience what rest as worship feels like.

The first picture: Sara comes from Sweden. The winters there are long, dark and cold, and come February or March, our bodies and souls begin to crave the sunlight as our D-vitamin stores are depleted. Even if you're from sunny old England you might relate to this feeling. Then comes the day when the world seems lighter than the day before, and someone says in shock "it's actually quite warm out there". And so you hurry outside and simply turn your face into the sunshine. You don't need to talk about it, explain to the sun what you need from it - nothing is asked of you in that moment. You simply follow the deep longing in your body and soul and place yourself where that longing can be met. Perhaps rest, and worship, are God's invitation to follow the deep longing in your body and soul, to place yourself where he can meet that need.

Or, let's try another picture: My friend was staying over in our house with her 2-year old. I so enjoyed hanging out with this little kid - there were abundant giggles and jokes, great picture books were shared and I constantly marvelled at the songs and ideas that came out of this tiny, cute human being. On the last day, he had just woken up from his afternoon nap and his mother had plonked him on our sofa while getting on with packing her bags. I thought I ought to help with childcare and so sat down next to him, waiting to see what kind of activity he'd initiate. But, perhaps because he was still sleepy and there was nothing either of us really needed to do in that moment, we just sat there. No chats, no jokes, no whining, no food requests, no stories required. My big grown-up body next to his tiny and warm little-boy body, simply sitting there in peace. And I just knew in that moment that this is how my Father God likes being with me, too. He likes my funny antics and when I try my best to use my gifts and when I get on with his other children. But I think he loves it when I just sit in his presence, no striving, no requests, no string of carefully curated words. Just my heart at rest, in a state of worship, right near to his Father-heart.

A final image: think about the love between two people. In any relationship, learning to communicate is crucial. We each express and receive love in different ways - for some, a thoughtful gift expresses love while it leaves others cold, and so on. We need to get to know each other to know how the other person best receives love. But crucially, *the gift is not the love*, it's a sign pointing towards the love. The spoken words "I love you" communicate *something* of the love, but it's not *the* love; at the end of the day, they are just words. It's the same with worship - all the activities of worship are good, but they are only signs pointing towards the worship. The worship is not the work we do, the words we say, the gifts we offer - worship is a state that our hearts are in. When we rest, we become most aware of the state of our hearts, most able to offer that unadorned gift of our presence and attention to the God who loves us.

You are not a device

Most books about rest start with a burn-out story. "I was a driven, successful, Type-A leader / professional / artist / human. I burned out and this is my story of recovery."

If you're burned out or feeling close to it; pull up a sofa, you're so welcome. But rest is not only about rehabilitating the broken, or recharging our dangerously depleted resources.

We all know that feeling: you glance at the battery icon on your phone, tablet or laptop, and it glares back at you with a red warning - battery low. Charge now! So you scurry around to find the right kind of cable to charge it up again, breathing a little deeper when it's back in that safe 100% place.

Our lives are so surrounded by technology that we assume that we, humans, are a bit like battery-driven devices. We expend our energy, not stopping until we get a red warning light (dropping off to sleep at the wheel, snapping at our loved ones, yawning uncontrollably during an important meeting, or more serious symptoms of exhaustion). Only then do we think to rest, or we might say "recharge". We think that a few extra hours in bed, or a box-set binge, or a spa weekend will refill our energy tank and set us off going again.

The problem is, you and I are not devices. We're not battery-driven technology. We are humans. We survive on more than bread, water and sleep alone. Rest is not simply a time to regain our energy, but the invitation to be *restored*, to be renewed, to be fundamentally changed from the inside out. It's an invitation into a deeper relationship with Jesus.

Reflect:

As you begin this journey, spend some time with the words on the next page from Christian medical doctor, Saundra Dalton-Smith.[1]

---

1   Saundra Dalton-Smith MD, *Sacred Rest,* (Faith Words, 2017) page 109-110.

"It is time to go back to the beginning when rest was required, when rest was sacred. When quietness was not a weakness and trust was not something to fear. Where we saw them for what they are, needed ingredients of a life worth living. Return to rest, quietness, and truth as a deer returns to a stream. Return to the source of your strength, and in doing so, you will be saved. Rest is salvation."

Saundra Dalton-Smith, Sacred Rest

Chapter 2
Our Story

Everyone has a lockdown story, and each story is different, but they all involve some level of upheaval, disruption, and re-assessment of life. When the COVID-19 pandemic shut down the UK in March 2020, our work with Engage Worship changed overnight. Suddenly all our training events and live worship services were cancelled. But we quickly discovered that churches were hungry for the kinds of resources we could provide for them online - family prayer ideas, video worship songs and reflective things which could be done in the home and over Zoom. We threw ourselves into creating more of these kinds of things. This then transitioned into another busy period of writing and producing six different resource books in just under two years.

As we in Engage Worship were finishing up the last of our six books in 2021, we gathered with our colleagues and trustees to pray and seek God for what was next. The only word that came through clearly to all of us was simply: *rest*. This seemed counterintuitive - now was a time when churches were getting back into meeting together. Shouldn't we focus on live training events? More new resources? Innovative projects?

As much as we tried, we couldn't shake the idea of "rest" out of our heads. We started reading all kinds of books on themes like rest, fun, play, and contemplative spirituality. We began reflecting on how rest was perhaps the missing piece in how churches approach gathered worship. But most of all, our gracious God was whispering in our ears: "Sara and Sam - *rest*. Don't just read about rest, think about rest, create resources around rest. I'm inviting you to *find rest.*"

As it turned out, we really needed that rest. Not because we were burned out or dangerously tired, but because in responding to God's invitation to rest we met with Jesus again. He began to strip away all the things we thought were so important (even things like leading worship, creating resources and writing songs), and point us towards the abundant life all around us. His gentle, kind love began to transform us from the inside out, reminding us who we truly are.

St Luke's Story

Remember back in Lockdown One when walks were our only social events? Early in the pandemic, Sam went on a walk with our friend, Revd Grace Sentamu Baverstock. It was quite a long walk and at one point they nearly got lost on a golf course. They chatted about worship, and how the disruption of COVID-19 was giving churches a chance to pause and reassess. Grace shared that she felt her church and her services had been too busy, too packed with activity. She was inspired by the way that simplified online services were connecting with her congregation, and they wondered aloud how churches could reimagine worship in a post COVID-19 world. This conversation led to a podcast, *Disrupting Worship*, where we chatted to worship leaders and pastors about what God might be saying to his church during this season.[1]

Around Easter 2022 we ended up joining Grace's church, St Luke's Leagrave. As the world gingerly emerged from lockdown, she had been putting a lot of our musings from the walks and the podcast into action. All of the services were radically shorter. The rotas were mostly scrapped but a wider range of people were being involved in leadership. Activity was limited to the bare essentials. She was prioritising rest, recovery and her relationship with God, and encouraging the congregation to do the same. And yet, remarkably, as the church focused on simplicity and rest, attendance on Sundays was growing in ways that the fellowship hadn't seen in years. As regular and active members of this church, we are now seeing the fruit of rest in worship right before our eyes.[2]

Reading this book

We've written this book with the aim that anyone can read it, at whatever pace works for you. There are 40 short chapters which means you could read it daily during Lent. Alternatively, feel free to dip in more sporadically at other times of the year, or binge the whole lot in a weekend!

---

1 engageworship.org/disrupting-worship
2 We unpack our experience at St Luke's further in Chapter 35.

Some of you are reading this book as pastors or worship leaders. We think that the gift of rest has very practical applications for church life, in particular how we organise, plan and lead restful gathered worship. Part 4 of this book will start to unpack some of these ideas. Our *Leaders' Resource eBook*[3] will provide you with more concrete ideas and suggestions that you can adapt for your church context and also contains an outline for running a six week *The Rest Is Worship* series in your services. However, you may want to resist the temptation to skip to those parts first.

When you get on an aeroplane, the safety announcement reminds you "In the unlikely event of a sudden loss of cabin pressure, oxygen masks will drop down from the panel above your head... secure your own mask before attending to others". This is the truth we've been learning slowly yet surely - if we want to lead others into the rest of God, we need to *fit our own masks first*. We need to enter into that rest for ourselves.

Before we can work out how to lead worship that is restful, God's rest needs to permeate our existence, impacting how we wake up in the morning, how we live with our families and friends, how we approach work and voluntary roles, how we think about holidays and time off. It touches on tender subjects such as how we feel about being alone, how we feel about ourselves when we're not being "useful", our comfort levels with silence, and how we deal with those awkward thoughts and emotions which surface when we're not being busy in order to ignore them.

---

3   engageworship.org/RestLeaders

Part 1 of this book explores God's *Invitation To Rest*. What is this gift Jesus is offering us, and how can our heart posture change towards being still? Part 2 focuses on *Rhythms Of Rest*, looking at how regular patterns of pausing can be incorporated into our daily, weekly and yearly cycles of work, family and other commitments. Part 3 delves into *A Restful Life*: what rest can look like in practice once we have paused, and how these restful activities are in themselves glorifying to God. Then Part 4 will address directly the subject of *Rest In Gathered Worship*: the invitation to a kind of church worship that includes more simplicity, stillness and receiving.

Treat this book as an invitation from Jesus to journey deeper into rest. As Ruth Haley Barton puts it:

> "It is a winsome call from this intriguing person we call God - the One who loves us, the One who is inexplicably drawn to us, the One who knows so intimately what we need in order to be well. It is an invitation straight from the heart of Jesus to us."[4]

As you read, try things out: new ways of praying, different rhythms for your day and week, fresh ways of looking at yourself, God, and the world around you. Deal with your own mask first - breathe deeply the life-giving breath of the Holy Spirit. Know the presence of Jesus, your Prince of Peace. Sit quietly beside the Father who loves you, and know that he receives your attention as worship.

---

4   Ruth Haley Barton, *Invitation to Retreat*, (InterVarsity Press, 2018) page 3.

Chapter 3
The Invitation

Imagine that you get a message like this from a close friend:

Hey!

You remember that house I've been working on? Guess what: it's all finished. The work is *done*. And if I say so myself, it's looking pretty amazing! Beautiful, practical, fully stocked up, everything we need for life in abundance. And now that I've finished all the work, I can begin the thing I made it for in the first place - enjoying it with the people I love.

So, I was wondering if you'd like to come and spend some time with me there? We can rest, have fun, be creative, enjoy the house, the garden, the lake, eat some great food... and you know, just *be* together for a bit. No stressy work, no striving, no burdensome responsibilities, no emails or social media...

Doesn't that sound good? Would you like that? Let me know, much love.

How would you feel about receiving that invitation - excited? Privileged? Blessed? Well, if that's the case, have you ever considered that this is the kind of invitation God has extended to *you*? That this is what God has in mind when he offers you the gift of rest?

In Genesis we read that God made a beautiful, abundant world. When he'd finished making it he began a day of rest (Gen 2:1-3), although not because he was exhausted - God doesn't get tired (Is 40:28). It is fair to surmise that he began that rest not for recovery but because he wanted to enjoy what he had made; he wanted to take pleasure in his creation. Notice too that this day doesn't end with "and there was evening, and there was morning", leading commentators to conclude that this day is an *eternal* day.[1] God invites the people that he made and loves to join him in that eternal rest; to enjoy the world in God's company. To just *be* with him. Forever.

Adam and Eve were created and invited to be with God in the garden, to live with him, to spend restful days with him. As Augustine expressed it in his *Confessions:* "You have made us for yourself, O Lord, and our hearts are restless until they rest in you."

In the gospels, Jesus invites us to "remain" or "abide" in him

---

1   FF Bruce, *The New International Commentary on the New Testament: The Epistle to the Hebrews*, (Eerdmans, 1990) page 106; Ben Witherington III, *The Rest of Life*, (Eerdmans, 2012) page 4.

(John 15:4-7). Abide is a word related to "abode": to make a home with. To truly worship God is to make our home in him, to spend our lives and our eternity responding to his offer of joyful, abundant relationship. Ben Quash writes in his book *Abiding*:

> "Worship is being with God, and being with each other in being with God."[2]

In worship it is God who invites and we who respond by choosing to abide, to be present with God and one another. The invitation before us is to come and enter into the rest God has provided for us - a lifetime and an eternity of truly *being* with him.

For many of us, this is what worship and Christian activities may have felt like in the early days of our faith. We may have read the Bible eager to spend time with its Author, unencumbered by the complexities of hermeneutics or ethics. We may have sung worship songs out of a desire simply to seek God's presence rather than being concerned with how in-tune our music was. We may have engaged in church and ministry and creativity for the joy of expressing our faith with others, not out of obligation, ambition or expectation.

Somewhere along the line, however, striving creeps in. Good things (education, goals, other people's opinions, paid roles, etc.) begin to nudge out this sense of restfully abiding in God's presence. Worship and the Christian life become a place of striving. As Ruth Haley Barton puts it, the devotional life becomes "a tool to accomplish utilitarian purposes rather than experiencing them as

---

2   Ben Quash, *Abiding*, (Bloomsbury Continuum, 2012) page 81.

a place of intimacy with God for my own soul's sake."[3]

Rest is an invitation to turn from striving and come back to the heart of God. It's a gift of abiding in God. It's an opportunity to be in relationship with God, to simply *be* in his presence, enjoying the world and the people around us.

Make this prayer your own:

Creator God,
open my eyes to your invitation.
Show me what it means to rest in you,
to be with you,
to enjoy you and the world you made.
Amen.

---

3   Ruth Haley Barton, *Sacred Rhythms*, (InterVarsity Press, 2006) page 47.

Chapter 4
Be Still

Given how most Christians live, you might think that the secret to a life in God is trying harder. Moving faster. Singing more energetically. Doing more service and ministry. It turns out that the word "workaholic" was first coined to describe a phenomenon observed in a study of pastors.[1] Makes sense…

Even when it comes to worship, we often operate under the maxim that "more is more". Bigger choirs. Louder bands. Greater stimulation through screens, lights and fast-moving services. It's as if we've found a bit in the Bible that says:

> Be more busy and know that I am God.
> Be louder and know that I am God.
> Strive harder and know that I am God.

But that's not actually what Psalm 46 says, is it?

In order that we might know him, God says that we are to "be

---

1   Alex Soojung-Kim Pang, *Rest*, (Penguin, 2018) page 164.

still". Some translations have "be silent", "stop striving", and even "calm down"!

What would it look like in your life, in your church, to take seriously God's invitation to be still? To stop striving, stressing, rushing? To be silent. Just to *be* with God.

Try this for a moment: get comfortable. Read the first line on the following page and then just breathe slowly for a moment. When you're ready, read the next line. Continue like this, with no other intention than just to be in God's presence.

Be still and know that I am God.

Be still and know that I Am.

Be still and know.

Be still.

Be.

How did that feel? Peaceful? Restful? Still? Or maybe nagging thoughts came into your head. "Isn't this a waste of time?" "Is this some dodgy form of praying?" "Did I leave the cooker on?"... If you experienced any of those distractions, welcome to being human.

Even so, the still, small voice of God speaks through all our noise: be still and *know that I am God*. Pausing, resting and being still are primarily about *knowing God*. God wants to be with us. He wants us not just to know *about* him but to know him. This is worship.

And one more thing: if *God* is God, then you and I are *not God*. The idolatry (false worship) of thinking that we're in charge, we're the ones making everything happen, that the world revolves around us, is broken by being still.

One of the problems with the busyness and hurry of modern church is that we can start to believe that we are, in fact, God. We start to think that we're indispensable. This person needs me. That church group can't live without me. I must comment on that social media post. I must pray for that thing. I must sing that song. *I must not stop.*

Henri Nouwen writes this about prayer, but it can apply to all worship:

> "Prayer is not a way of being busy with God instead of with people. In fact, it unmasks the illusion of busyness, usefulness and indispensability. It is a way of being empty and useless in the presence of God and so of proclaiming

our basic belief that all is grace and nothing is simply
the result of hard work... Prayer as an articulate way of
being useless in the face of God brings a smile to all we do
and creates humour in the midst of our occupations and
preoccupations."[1]

How do you feel about that - being "empty and useless"? For
some, "useless" has connotations of being without value, but I
think Nouwen means to stop striving, pausing from trying to earn
our value by achieving things, resting from trying to be God and
instead knowing that God is God. Trusting that God is in control,
and that if I rest, if I am still, he will keep the world spinning. He
will look after my loved ones, my church, my work.

And I love that last line - that when we rest it "brings a smile
to all we do and creates humour". Have you ever noticed that?
There are two very different modes of doing things - we can work
and minister and live in an anxious, stressed out, begrudging way
(like the elder brother of the prodigal son). Or, if we have given
ourselves over to God's rest, we can do all the same tasks and
engage in the same interactions but do so with an attitude of joy,
of lightness, of peace, with a genuine smile and humour because
we trust that God is in control.

Respond:

Repeat the "Be Still" exercise once more.

---

1   Henri Nouwen, *The Living Reminder* in *Making All Things New and Other Classics*,
(Zondervan, 2000) page 262.

Chapter 5
Getting Better at Rest

We - Sam and Sara - used to think we knew how to rest. However over the past few years we've sensed God saying he wants to teach us, as individuals and as a family, how to rest *better*. God has been doing rest since the seventh day of creation (and presumably an eternity before that), so he's something of an expert. But is rest something you can improve at? Can you rest in more or less godly, healthy, life-giving ways?

Alex Soojung-Kim Pang writes this about rest:

> "Everyone basically knows how to do it, but with a little work and understanding, you can learn to do it a lot better. You can enjoy rest more profoundly and be more refreshed and restored."[1]

He goes on to say that this can sound counterintuitive - surely rest is like breathing, or standing still. Isn't it a natural thing we do

---

1   Alex Soojung-Kim Pang, *Rest*, (Penguin, 2018) page 14.

innately, something we picked up as a child and just do without thinking? How could we improve something so instinctive?

I recently started going to a singing teacher. My voice was getting tired when I sang, and I wanted to improve my pitch and tone. What surprised me was that she didn't begin by focusing on things like scales or arpeggios. We didn't sing a lot of songs, or do any of the "advanced" singing techniques I thought she might major on. Instead, she began with two basic things I do without thinking: breathing and standing!

It turns out for my entire adult life I had been breathing all wrong. Who knew? Somewhere along the line I'd got into some seriously bad habits in the way I took a breath before singing. Similarly, my hunched posture was trapping the notes inside my body and causing all sorts of tuning and tone problems.

I needed to start being mindful of two things that I took completely for granted - how I stood, and how I breathed. Being intentional in these very basic areas has improved my vocal health and performance in remarkable ways.

The same can be said of rest. If we approach it mindlessly, falling into our usual and instinctive habits (TV binges, an over-reliance on alcohol or comfort eating, endless social media scrolling, poor sleep patterns, trying to throw money at the problem... etc.) we will often find that what we count as "rest" does not truly restore us. We might call this "Counterfeit Rest", the rest promised to us by tech companies, advertisements and our instinctive coping mechanisms.

The good news is, Jesus has so much more for us.

> "Come to me, all you who are weary and burdened, and I
> will give you rest. Take my yoke upon you and learn from
> me, for I am gentle and humble in heart, and you will find
> rest for your souls. For my yoke is easy and my burden is
> light." (Matt 11:28-30)

Jesus invites you to come to him so that he can "show you how
to take a real rest" (Matt 11:28 MSG). Real rest, not Counterfeit
Rest. Rest that reaches your truest needs. Rest tailored to your
current situation and individual character type. Rest that restores
your heart, soul, mind and strength. Rest that honours God, and
is worship to God.

As we have journeyed deeper into this invitation for ourselves, we
have had to re-learn what felt like some very basic skills. What
does it mean to take a day off? How do I wake in the morning
in a way that embraces God's rest? How do I prepare myself for
bed in the evening? What is a restful prayer life supposed to look
like? How do I relate to the demands of family, work, church and
community?

At times this has felt like going back to nursery school, yet Jesus is
a kind and generous teacher. He doesn't use shame, fear or ridicule
to try to force us to change. Instead he says "learn from me, for I
am gentle and humble in heart" (Matt 11:29). We have a teacher
who is gentle and humble, not arrogantly standing over us, but
getting alongside us. He leads us into his rhythms of grace, his
green pastures where our souls, minds and bodies can be restored.

This journey will involve practical steps, tips and life-hacks. There are decisions to make, ways of organising your life, your church involvement and other things. But at its core, the journey of rest is about one thing: coming to Jesus. Hear this invitation to you today:

> "Come to me, all you who are weary and burdened, and I will give you rest."

Reflect:

Look at the words of *Come All You Heavy Laden* on the next page. If you like, listen to the song.[2] Ask Jesus to lead you into the true rest he has for you.

---

2   © Timo Scharnowski, Sam Hargreaves, admin by ChurchSongs.co.uk
CCLI # 7212312. Listen here - engageworship.org/ComeAllYou

Come all you heavy laden.
Come all you broken down.
Come all your burned and fragile,
find rest for your souls.

Come all you stressed and anxious.
Come all who clench their fists.
Come all whose minds are reeling,
find rest for your souls.

Peace, be still, my soul.
Hear the words of Jesus.
Come and sit at his feet,
come, it's all that you need.
Surrender all, be still my soul.

Jesus, your yoke is easy,
Jesus your burden's light.
You walk along beside me
in rhythms of grace.

Help me lay down my burdens,
help me unclench my fists.
Breathing a little deeper,
in rhythms of grace.

Timo Scharnowski, Sam Hargreaves

Chapter 6
Created for Work, Rest and Worship

Hollywood loves an origin story. Given half a chance, the movies will delve into how Batman became Batman, or how Princess Leia ended up with plans for the Death Star, or how Willy Wonka became crazy about chocolate. These stories are supposed to help us see *why* the characters act the way they do, explaining their reason for existence, their drives and motivations.

Genesis 1-3 is the origin story of the human race. In a limited number of dense, poetic words it paints a picture of God's intentions for us, why we exist and why we act in the ways we do.

We have already said that when God had finished creating, he rested (Gen 2:2), and that the people he created joined him in that rest. At the same time, he also invited them to work:

> "The Lord God took the man and put him in the Garden of Eden to work it and take care of it." (Gen 2:15)

Now bear in mind: this is before the Fall. So both the rest and the work at this stage are purely good and in keeping with the good creation. Work is not a curse, it is a gift. In Genesis 2, humanity works in fulfilling, creative and generative ways: naming the animals, cultivating the garden and the raw materials God provides.

Similarly, the gift of rest is joining with God in enjoying creation, delighting in one another, and basking in his presence as he walks with them in the cool of the day (Gen 3:8). Adam and Eve don't need to be *commanded* to rest at this stage, it is the most natural thing for them to enjoy the rest God is offering them.

Only after sin enters the picture do we see that work becomes hard, frustrating "toil" (Gen 3:17-19). This is also when rest becomes about "recovery" from the exhaustion of this toil. Today we live in this fallen world where work and rest are marred by sin and slog.

Can you relate to this? Do you ever look at your to-do list, that pile of dirty laundry, the spreadsheet you have to create or the difficult people you have to lead, and let out a groan? Has rest become about desperately trying to recharge your depleted batteries before another round of exhausting work? If so, you're not alone. And yet God's invitation to us is to rediscover what he originally intended work and rest to be: good and fulfilling gifts.

As well as being beautiful and life-giving gifts, work and rest are also invitations to worship. You see, when the humans are called to work in Genesis 2:15 the word for work is *abad*. This word is often translated as "worship" in other parts of the Old Testament. In fact, Gordon Wenham points out that this phrase is the same as the priest's job description in the temple, and that many of the features of Eden are later echoed in the designs of the tabernacle and Jerusalem temple.[1] So picture it: Eden was made by God as a place of perfect worship.

We were created to work, rest, and worship. In our fallen state, we tend to see those three things as distinct, almost competing categories. We can view work as the toil part of life, rest as the recharge from exhaustion, and worship as the spiritual bit we fit in the gaps. But that isn't what it was like in Eden: work and rest were good and not cursed; work was worship and rest was worship. John Mark Comer puts it like this:

> "Just like work, when it's done right, is an act of worship, the same is true with rest. You can rest as an act of worship to God. You can even rest to the glory of God. When you enjoy the world as God intended [...] in a spirit of gratitude, letting the goodness of your world and life conjure up an awareness of God and a love for him, then rest becomes worship."[2]

Back in 2017 we released a book called *Whole Life Worship*.[3] We explored how every aspect of our lives can bring glory to God, and how gathered worship in a church community can reflect that. As

---

1   Gordon Wenham, "Sanctuary Symbolism in the Garden of Eden Story", in *Proceedings of the World Congress of Jewish Studies* 9 (1986).

2   John Mark Comer, *Garden City*, (Zondervan, 2015) pages 197-198.

3   Sam & Sara Hargreaves, *Whole Life Worship*, (IVP 2017).

we've taught this material in countless workshops and seminars since then, we've often emphasised how every act of work can be offered to God as an act of worship. It has been exciting to see the change of perspective this can have for people. Formerly "meaningless", boring or difficult tasks can be re-envisioned as offerings of praise and glory to God, and ways of bringing his Kingdom on earth. God's intention for work in creation begins to shine through.

This book is, in some ways, adding a missing puzzle-piece to *Whole Life Worship*. Just as work can be worship, rest can also be worship. Stopping to rest is not about being lazy. It doesn't make us ineffective for the Kingdom, and it isn't supposed to be put off until we're exhausted. When we rest with God, we are fulfilling part of his intention in creating us. When we rest with God, we are giving him glory and praise.

Pray:

Hold your hands out in front of you, and picture the things you do for work held in your hands. Lift them up to God, offering them back to him as worship.

Then picture the things you do to rest held in your hands: days off, hobbies, quiet times, walks, sleep… whatever counts as rest for you. Again, lift these things up to God, asking him to lead you deeper into how these can bring him glory and praise.

Chapter 7
The Work, Rest and Worship to Come

Just as work, rest and worship are integral to our origin story, we also find them in the grand finale of the story of God. We need to know where we've come from, but we also need to know where we're going. If Genesis is the origin story, the book of Revelation is the all-singing-all-dancing climax, showing us what eternity with God has in store.

Revelation 14:13 says that the dead "will rest from their labour, for their deeds will follow them." Right there we see the promise of eternal rest, and also the idea that our deeds (or this can be interpreted as our "occupations") will accompany us into the new heavens and new earth.[1] So eternity won't mean simply sitting around being bored, but the fulfilment of both rest and of our work.

---

1 See John Mark Comer, *Garden City*, (Zondervan, 2015) pages 260-264.

Later in chapters 21 and 22 we see a glorious picture of the new Jerusalem as a garden city on a restored earth, with the promise: "No longer will there be any curse" (Rev 22:1-3). No more curse refers back to the problem we identified in the previous chapter: work and rest will no longer be tainted by the Fall.

In God's renewed creation all work will be what God intended: fulfilling, creative, generative. Rest will no longer be recovery from the exhaustion of toil but instead a delighted freedom to enjoy God and all his gifts. And the passage goes on to say: "the throne of God and of the Lamb will be there, and his servants will worship him. And they will see his face" (22:3-4, NLT). What a picture: worshipping God the Father and Jesus, not at a distance but face-to-face! Truly this is the promise of Eden fulfilled for eternity.

Sabbath

We know that between the garden of Eden and the garden city of Revelation, rest and work are cursed. And yet God graciously makes provision for his people to rest: the gift of the Sabbath day. Sabbath is a beautiful invitation to join with the God who rested at creation (Ex 20:11) and who will welcome us into eternal rest (Heb 4:9-11).

We talk about our own rediscovery of Sabbath practice in Chapter 28. It has been life-giving for us as a family, and is much needed in our restless world. Yet it is also true that it is easy to become legalistic about the Sabbath.

The Pharisees exhibited the epitome of this kind of behaviour.

Throughout Jesus' ministry we see him constantly jostling against the many extra rules they had placed around the Sabbath. They want him to stay within their strict boundaries; he wants to bring life in abundance. Jesus ends up telling them that the Sabbath was made for humans, not humans for the Sabbath, or in one translation:

> "The Sabbath was made to meet the needs of people, and not people to meet the requirements of the Sabbath." (Mark 2:27 NLT)

Jesus shows us that Sabbath isn't meant to be an exercise in obeying complex requirements. It has a *function*: it meets our needs in terms of reminding us, on a regular basis, that we are not God, that human achievement is not ultimate, that we are not enslaved to commerce, that rest is good, and so on.

But as well as a function, Sabbath also has a *symbolism*. Our Sabbath today points us towards a deeper truth: the eternal rest of God. This rest is the promise of the coming Kingdom of God; the restoration of all things; the renewed heaven and earth we read about earlier in Revelation. It is a rest that has been begun in Christ but that we will not see in its fullness until Christ comes again. Ben Witherington III writes:

> "The older we get, the easier we tire, the more we need our rest. But this very condition should daily remind us that we are being prepared for a better rest, a bigger rest, indeed for God's rest. The ordinary rest reminds us of the extraordinary one we have only a foretaste of now, but will

fully enjoy later when Kingdom comes."[2]

Looking at work, rest and worship in this light is transformative. We still live in a fallen world. Our bodies and our bad habits still need the rhythm of work days and Sabbath days. But it's not just an end in itself: it's a foretaste and a dragging-into-now of the eternal rest and worship that is to come.

Reflect:

Keiko Ying's wonderful song *Lord of the Sabbath* does a great job of holding together both how Sabbath helps us in our fallen world, and also how Sabbath points us towards the ultimate rest Jesus promises for eternity. We have printed verses one and four below for you to reflect on. You can also listen to the full song online.[3]

> Lord of the Sabbath, here we confess
> hearts that are restless - though hands are at rest -
> with relentless accusing of things left undone;
> Lord of the Sabbath, have mercy on us.
>
> Lord of the Sabbath, Jesus our hope,
> soon you'll return to restore the whole world
> bringing ultimate rest to your dearest belov'd;
> Lord, of the Sabbath have mercy on us.

---

2   Ben Witherington III, *The Rest of Life*, (Eerdmans, 2012) page 29.

3   © Keiko Ying. Listen here - engageworship.org/redirect/LordSabbath
For more of Keiko's music visit https://keikoeying.wixsite.com/website

Chapter 8
What Will You Find?

> "Our willingness to rest depends on what we believe we will find there. At rest, we come face-to-face with the essence of life. If we believe life is fundamentally good, we will seek our rest as a taste of that goodness. If we believe life is fundamentally bad or flawed, we will be reluctant to quiet ourselves, afraid of meeting the darkness that resides in things - or ourselves."[1]

In a world of infinite distractions, the idea of true rest can be terrifying. We may worry that when the busyness subsides, the noise fades, the devices are switched off and there's nobody else around, we may not like what we find. We may fear the negative thoughts that will rise up, uncovering uncomfortable truths about ourselves, the world, or God. Or perhaps we are nervous of finding that when we are still and quiet, all that is left is just a resounding, hopeless silence?

---

1   Wayne Muller, *Sabbath*, (Bantam, 2000) page 40.

Silence, solitude and stillness can be scary. But they can also be the places where we hear the deepest whispers of God:

I love you. I love this world. My plans for you are good.

It is important to root ourselves in Genesis 1 and 2, where God makes the heavens and the earth and he calls them *good*. This world is fundamentally good. God so loves this world (John 3:16).

God makes humankind, woman and man in his image, and he calls us *very good*. At your core, you are very good. Often our theology can start with Genesis 3 (the Fall) rather than Genesis 1 and 2. Sin mars the image of God in us, but it doesn't destroy it. We may have defaced the masterpieces God made us to be, but we haven't completely ruined them. You are made in the image of God. God made you good.

Reflect:

How easy do you find it to believe that God made you and called you very good? That the deepest truth of your life is that God loves you?

Revealing God

A friend told me recently that she grew up afraid of God. She could only imagine God as angry, vengeful, constantly picking up on her every mistake. In her adult years, she stopped going to church and drifted away from faith. Then one day, during a tough time in her life, she wandered into a different fellowship. She was overwhelmed by the God she met there - a God of love, of acceptance, a good God who always protects, always trusts, always hopes, always perseveres with us (1 Cor 13:7). This encounter transformed her life, and she has followed and served this God of love fruitfully ever since. This is the God revealed to us in Jesus.

Jesus is "the image of the invisible God" (Col 1:15), "the radiance of God's glory and the exact representation of his being" (Heb 1:3). Jesus shows us definitively what God is like. And ultimately, the picture we get from Jesus is that *God is love* (1 John 4:16).

In the gospels, there are three times when God the Father speaks with an audible voice, and twice he says almost exactly the same thing:

> [At Jesus' baptism] "a voice from heaven said, 'This is my Son, whom I love; with him I am well pleased.'" (Matt 3:17)

> [At the transfiguration] "a voice from the cloud said, 'This is my Son, whom I love; with him I am well pleased. Listen to him!'" (Matt 17:5)

When the curtain is pulled back on heaven, we hear the deepest truth: *Abba* loves the Son, delights in him, is well pleased with him. God exists in eternal love as Father, Son and Spirit.

A few years ago I preached on these passages, and said that what God says over Jesus he also speaks over us. Two separate people came up to me afterwards and they both said the same thing: "I agree with you when you say God loves us, but I'm not sure about God being pleased with us." I guess they were thinking: when God looks at me, he sees my sin, he sees my mistakes, my frailties.

How can he say "with you I am well pleased"?

When God looks at us, people adopted by his Spirit as daughters and sons, he sees us as his precious children in Christ.

> "For those who are led by the Spirit of God are the children of God. [...] the Spirit you received brought about your adoption to sonship. And by him we cry, '*Abba*, Father.' The Spirit himself testifies with our spirit that we are God's children." (Rom 8:14-16)

When God looks at his children, he sees the perfection of Jesus in us. In Christ we are new creations - the old has gone (2 Cor 5:17). He sees the new you, the true you, the you that he intended when he made you. We can call out to him using that same intimate name Jesus did: "*Abba*". He responds to you speaking the same words he spoke over Jesus: *You are my daughter, my son, I love you, I delight in you, I am pleased with you.* Can you receive that for yourself?

Being still, resting, has at its heart the invitation to enter into that truth. To know the God who knows you, who loves you, who accepts you.

Pray:

Take some time to sit in stillness, and simply ask "God, show me how you love me." It may not be immediate or dramatic, but as you let other noises subside allow yourself to become aware of God's love for you.

Chapter 9
Yield

"Yes, I'll rest when..." Fill in the blank for yourself:

> ... I've finished this project.
> ... the kids are through this stage.
> ... I've handed in my essay.
> ... my business starts to make a profit.
> ... I finally feel satisfied...

The problem is, of course, that even if you do ever finish that thing, something else always pops up, and so you put off resting again, and again. In church and worship ministry this can be particularly difficult, because our goals are so lofty: see our whole town come to Jesus! Unite the diverse congregations in song so that nobody complains! Build up a thriving music worship ministry! Just as you think you're making progress, a key worship leader leaves for university or a new job, or your PA system goes on the blink, or a "cooler" church opens up down the road.

One of the beautiful gifts that God gives us in the Sabbath is a picture of rest which does not wait until we're "finished". Sabbath interrupts our work. It breaks into our sense of "achieving things". It reminds us to pause even when our work is far from done.

In Sara's native Sweden, there is a beloved comic book based around the character Bamse, the "World's Strongest Bear". One of the main characters is Skalman, the tortoise who carries an alarm clock everywhere he goes to remind him to nap at regular intervals. It doesn't matter how perilous an adventure Bamse and the gang find themselves in - whatever is going on around him, Skalman will hear that alarm and immediately go to sleep! Everyone else generally panics in response, but inevitably it will turn out that Skalman's rest doesn't stop them overcoming the problem, and in fact his pauses are often instrumental in their victory.

One way of looking at rest is to think about the idea of "yielding". Rest is a moment to say: I'm not going to achieve everything in my timescale. I'm choosing to let go of control. I'm deciding to leave things unfinished, to leave them in the hands of our loving, trustworthy God, and to rest in the midst of incompleteness.

In the UK we have "Give Way" signs on our roads, that instruct the driver to slow down and give priority to the other traffic. In the USA the same kind of signs just say "Yield". When we yield, we give someone else priority. We accept their right of way. We say "not my will, but your will be done."

To yield can feel like a defeat. It brings to my mind old-time duels where one party was wounded and the other would ask "do you yield?", meaning, do you surrender, do you accept that you have lost? To yield to someone else's opinion, instruction or demand can feel like giving up, failing, being vanquished.

But yield, as well as being a verb, is also a noun, indicating fruitfulness and generosity. At harvest time the fields produce a "yield" of crops. A financial investment can return a "yield" of money. Both the noun and verb senses of the word have their root in the Old English *gield*, meaning "payment, sum of money; service, offering, worship".[1] So to yield is to submit, and yet at the same time this surrender can lead to us being actively fruitful, and can ultimately yield a service of worship to God.

This is why Jesus' prayer in Gethsemane is one of the most remarkable acts of worship ever recorded. In the darkest hour of his life so far, when he knows he is about to be betrayed, falsely convicted and brutally killed, he is sweating blood in fear, confusion and anxiety. And yet, at this moment, he prays:

> "*Abba*, Father, for you all things are possible; remove this cup from me; yet, not what I want, but what you want."
> (Mark 14:36)

Note first that he acknowledges God as both his intimate *Abba*, and also the almighty one for whom all things are possible. In this moment, Jesus yields to who his Father is.

Secondly, he offers up how he feels and what he instinctively wants. He effectively says "if there is any other way, I'll take that

---

1 www.etymonline.com/word/yield

instead." We can be honest with God in prayer and worship. We can tell him how we feel, and what we want, even if we suspect our "wants" are not ultimately the best.

Finally, Jesus yields completely. It is not about what he wants, it's about what God his Father wants. He trusts himself entirely to his loving Father. He trusts that as he yields, seemingly in defeat, that ultimately this sacrifice will provide a rich harvest, and it will resound across eternity as the supreme act of worship to the glory of God.

Reflect:

What are your current goals: for your life, your family, work? What are your goals for the church ministry you're involved in? How do you feel about pausing, resting, while those goals are still left unachieved? Reflect on what it would look like to yield and trust those things to God.

Chapter 10
Martha

There is a way of teaching the Martha and Mary story (Luke 10:38-42) - and teaching about rest and worship in general - that is deeply guilt-inducing. "Stop being a Martha and be a Mary!" is not necessarily what is said, but it is often what we hear. And it easily puts our backs up. Doesn't Jesus know all the demands on us? If we don't feed the kids / lead the team / work on that spreadsheet / care for that sick person / prepare that service (etc...) who else is going to do it? It's all very well for *other* people to take time out, to rest, to spend endless time with Jesus, but some of us need to keep the wheels turning around here...

And deeper than that, we have the fear that if we relate to Martha, perhaps we're the "wrong kind of person" for Jesus. Does he love the Marys more than the Marthas? Are those who instinctively plan, act, work, organise and get things done less attractive to Jesus than the ones who just sit at his feet, singing gentle worship songs for hours or meditating in monasteries for most of their lives?

This is why I love Hannah Hodges' song, which imagines Jesus addressing Martha (see the lyrics on page 46). Hannah captures what I think is the true heart of this complex relationship.

We need to remember that Jesus had a special bond with the siblings at Bethany. Jesus could have stayed in many places, but he seems to have a particular soft spot for the company of Martha, Mary and Lazarus. In fact, John tells us plainly: "Now Jesus loved Martha and her sister and Lazarus." (John 11:5). He *loved* Martha. He had deep affection for her. He saw her as she was, he valued her character.

This is evident at the grave of Lazarus (John 11:17-37). We know that with Mary, Jesus simply weeps, drawing alongside her in her grief. But it is also highly significant to see the way Jesus relates to Martha at this moment. She has questions; deep, theological, practical questions, and Jesus is prepared to engage with her in them. He values her enquiring mind and her pragmatic concern - will my brother rise again? Jesus enters into this discussion with her, revealing his true identity as the resurrection and the life.

This is important, because it re-frames how we view the Luke 10 passage. If Jesus loved and valued Martha, he wasn't annoyed that she was serving him food. And he certainly didn't love Mary more than Martha. Martha might have entertained this idea herself: notice how she says to Jesus: "Lord, don't you care that my sister has left me to do the work by myself?" Don't you *care*? This bold question suggests that Martha had been aware of Jesus caring for her in the past, yet in this moment she is not so sure. How can Jesus let her work herself to the bone?

The key, I think, to going deeper with this story is the word "distracted" (Luke 10:40). Luke doesn't say "Martha mistakenly thought she had to prepare the food." The food actually needed preparing. That was an important task, and no doubt Martha was doing it with excellence.

The problem was, the good thing of food preparation was distracting her from the most important thing: being with Jesus. She had allowed herself to become worried and troubled (Luke 10:41), rather than doing her work with a lightness and joy. This led to resentment of her sister - a bitterness and indignation that she "had" to do all the work while Mary slacked off. And Martha (again to her credit) didn't push these feelings down - she boldly and directly addressed the issue to Jesus.

It is important to see Jesus' response through the eyes of his love for her. Imagine a situation where you see a dear friend working themselves into a frenzy over a project. What is, at heart, good and important work has begun to consume them, they are experiencing deep anxiety, and lashing out at the people around them. In this context, your role is not to tell them off, but to come alongside them with compassion, gently pointing out a better way which will restore health and peace to their soul.

The Passion paraphrase of this passage helps us enter into the loving way Jesus responds:

> "Martha, my beloved Martha. Why are you upset and troubled, pulled away by all these many distractions? Mary has discovered the one thing most important by choosing to

sit at my feet." (Luke 10:41-42 TPT)

This is not a rebuke to stop working, it's an invitation to let go of her anxieties at Jesus' feet. To take the time and space to re-prioritise, put first things first, see her work in its right perspective. It's an opportunity to remember that she loves her sister, and that in her best moments she would want nothing more for Mary than that she be at Jesus' feet. And most fundamentally, it is an invitation to be in the presence of Jesus and receive his love.

Reflect:

Spend some time with the lyrics of this song to Martha on the next page.[1] The second half of the lyrics are almost a stream of consciousness from God's heart to you. Let Jesus speak to you today (feel free to insert your own name in place of Martha's).

---

1 © Hannah Hodges, admin by ChurchSongs.co.uk CCLI # 7212383.
Listen here - engageworship.org/redirect/Martha

Martha, I love you and I see the work you've done,
it pleases me how much you serve everyone,
but don't forget that I'm right here.
Martha, put down your things and sit down at my feet,
don't give me the excuse you're too busy,
you can't pour from an empty cup.

So choose what's best,
here in my presence I'll give you rest.
All you need is found within your life with me.
Give me what you're carrying,
I know you find it hard to ask for help,
so let go, I'll take that weight upon myself.

Oh my love, be brave enough to recognise
that surrender isn't a weak thing,
submission isn't a dirty word,
you don't have to be in control all the time,
you are not the Holy Spirit
you're not responsible for other people's healing.
Oh leave it to me,
let me in and I will show you what it's like
to live freely and lightly.
Oh Martha come and rest.
Come and rest in my presence Martha.
Oh I love you I love you Martha
I love you I love you Martha,
my child.

Hannah Hodges

Part Two:

rhythms of rest

Chapter 11
Playing the Rests

Claude Debussy wrote that music is "the space between the notes", while Miles Davis said: "It's not the notes you play; it's the notes you don't play." That would suggest that in a musical score, more important than the crotchets, quavers and minims, are the rests. The *rest*.

In fact, on 29th August 1952, concert pianist David Tudor sat down at the piano in front of an audience and for four and a half minutes made no sound. He was performing a piece by composer John Cage called *4'33"* - a piece with no notes, just rests.

I don't know what you think about that. Some people have described it as "absolutely ridiculous", "stupid", "a gimmick", and "the emperor's new clothes."[1] Maybe. However, if you've ever been in a busy street, a noisy workplace, a chaotic home, or a loud, frantic church service, you might have welcomed a performance of *4'33"*.

---

1 See Alex Ross, *Listen To This*, (HarperCollins, 2011) page 266.

Right now it feels like God might be calling us to focus less on the notes and more on the *rests*. To learn how to rest. How to pause. How to introduce silence and stillness and simplicity back into our services, our worship, our lives. What would it look like to respond to God's challenge through Isaiah:

> "In repentance and rest is your salvation, in quietness and trust is your strength". (Is 30:15)

Of course, Cage's *4'33"* is an extreme example. In reality, most music is not made up of continuous rests. The majority of music is a combination of notes and gaps. Rests offer breathing space (for singers and wind players, literally) between phrases. The listener's ear picks up not only on the notes but on the gaps - the pauses which encourage you to listen out for more.

Listen:

Find a recording of Arvo Pärt's *Spiegel im Spiegel*.[2] Listen for the long gaps in the viola part as it rests on the simple, repeated piano. Pärt has said that Jesus Christ is the inspiration for his music, and this piece (the title translates as "a mirror in a mirror") points us to the rest of eternity. Spend time resting in the peace of this piece.

Musical rests are a great analogy for the rest God offers us in our lives. Activity, work, human interaction - these are good things, like the notes in a piece of music. But if we play all notes with no rests, musicians get exhausted, and our listeners' ears begin to zone out. Similarly, if our lives are all work but no rest, we get

---

2   You can stream it via engageworship.org/redirect/spiegel

tired. We lack the space to pause, reflect back on what has gone before and anticipate what is coming next.

Rests can look like the more extensive breaks of a holiday or residential retreat, or the day-long breaks of a Sabbath or day off. But they can also be much shorter - a moment to catch your breath, to become aware of how you are feeling and what is going on around you, to remind yourself of God's presence, to pause before moving on.

You'll remember the story of the woman caught in adultery in John 8. Jesus is put in an impossible situation by the Pharisees - if he acquits the woman he looks like he's ignoring the law of Moses. But if he agrees that she should be stoned, he violates the Roman law and the poor, entrapped woman will be killed. It seems that he just can't win.

In these kinds of situations when we're backed into a corner, "fight or flight" mode can kick in: we can become angry or violent, or just try to run away. But Jesus does neither. In fact, he does something a bit odd - he stoops down and draws in the sand. There are all kinds of theories as to why he did this, but one at least as good as all the others is that he was simply taking a pause. Bending down, he no longer had the smug, accusative eyes of the Pharisees on him. He could take a beat, breathe, remind himself of who he was and of God's heart of grace and love for this woman. By the time he straightens up, he has the perfect answer.

If we're going to follow Jesus in learning to pause, we will need to develop some habits, our own versions of "writing in the sand".

Here are some experiments to try for yourself:

Punctuate your day with grace. People pause to say "grace" before meals. It is a great example of a rest moment - but why stop with food? Could you pause and acknowledge God at other times? For example: when you leave the house; when you start a new work task or household chore; when you're about to have a difficult conversation with someone... a friend even suggested we pause to thank God for electricity each time we turn on a light! These are places where 30 seconds to pause, acknowledge God and commit the next task to him could make such a difference.

Mini-*examen*. *Examen* prayers, at their simplest, encourage us to reflect back on what was good and what was a challenge over a period of time.[3] Could you take one minute when you come to the end of a task or activity, instead of rushing on to the next thing, to ask those two questions? For example, when you finish reading a novel or listening to a podcast, doing a chore or having a conversation, stop and ask: what did I like about that? What did I find difficult about it? It may be that your reflections lead you towards prayers of praise, confession, asking for help, or simply admitting to God how you feel about something.

Pray:

Try a mini-*examen* now. What did you find helpful about this chapter? Talk to God about that. What was more difficult, challenging, or confusing? Talk to God about why you might have felt those things. Ask him to lead you into rhythms of rest.

---

3   We look more closely at *examen* in Chapter 38.

Chapter 12
Pausing to be Present

We live in a distracting world. There are more noises, lights, movement and activities than ever.

The issue with so much of this distraction is that we are very rarely *present*. We might be talking to a friend, spending time with our children, working on a task or trying to get some rest, but countless voices, alerts and demands will try to distract us. It becomes difficult to really focus on someone or something, to give the present moment our full attention. And even when we do find some peace and solitude, the continual whirring of our minds can cause us to remain absent - occupied with chewing over mistakes in the past, or pre-occupied with things we're worried might happen in the future.

In the movie version of this book, I see these distractions building on our hero's shoulders, dissonant sounds and voices piling on top of one another until the person is almost crushed and the cacophony is at the peak of its crescendo... then: PAUSE. A finger presses a pause button and the distractions stop suddenly. We all breathe again.

Part of God's invitation to rest is to press "pause" on distractions. That might be for a day, or an hour, or just five minutes. God invites us to say a calm but firm "no" to these things that steal our attention. And as we do so, we are offered the gift of becoming more present to ourselves, the moment we're in, and to God.

In the last chapter, we talked about John Cage's silent piano piece 4'33". Actually, it's a mistake to call it a silent piece, because while the musician doesn't play, the intention is really that the audience become more aware of the other sounds around them. Cage himself said of the premiere:

> "They missed the point. There's no such thing as silence. What they thought was silence, because they didn't know how to listen, was full of accidental sounds. You could hear the wind stirring outside during the first movement. During the second, raindrops began pattering the roof, and during the third the people themselves made all kinds of interesting sounds as they talked or walked out."[1]

Notice that - *they didn't know how to listen*. Or we might say, they didn't know how to be present to what was going on around them.

---

1   John Cage quoted in Richard Kostelanetz, *Conversing with Cage*, (Routledge, 2003) page 65.

Let's try an experiment:

Take a moment to look around the room or space you are in. Look more intently than you have before. Can you spot something you hadn't seen previously? Is there an area of beauty, brokenness or something else that appears when you take the time to be present?

Now close your eyes, be still and as quiet as you can. Try to identify all the sounds around you. What can you hear, close or far off? What do you become aware of that you weren't before?

Next, close your eyes again and become aware of your body. How are you feeling in yourself? Any aches and pains? Any tension? Do you feel energised, or lethargic, or something else?

Now finally, turn your attention to God. Jesus is with you, all the time, but we rarely pause to focus on him. What name or attribute would you use to describe Jesus right now, something you know him to be or need him to be to you today? Is he Prince of Peace, friend, great physician, Lion of Judah, water of life...? Say that name or attribute to him, and be aware of any response.

The gift of the present

The point of those exercises was to become present. You became aware of what you could see. You gave your attention to the sounds around you. You allowed yourself to feel your body. You thought about God and how he relates to you in this moment.

Rest is an opportunity to pause and be present. Present to ourselves - how am I really feeling? What's going on in my heart, in my mind, in my body, in my emotions? You're giving yourself time to reflect, and for some of us that is challenging because there are things inside of us we'd rather not reflect on. But God wants us to be real. He wants us to think through those things because that's how he can begin to work on them and heal them.

Rest is also an opportunity to be present to the world around us. To start to notice that tree or that ant, the sounds of birdsong and cars. To begin to see glimpses of God in the world he has made.

When we rest, we also begin to be present to other people. Practising rest can change the way we relate, and we begin to pay more attention to what our children, our spouse, or our friends are saying to us. We can spend time with them without rushing away.

And ultimately, we rest to be present to God.

Pray:

Listen to the recording of Sam's song, *Lead Me to a Place of Rest*.[2] The lyrics are on the next page if you want to reflect on them. As the song ends, sit silently with God, not trying to say prayers or achieve anything. Simply be present to God in this moment.

---

2 © Sam Hargreaves, admin by ChurchSongs.co.uk CCLI # 7212314. Listen here - engageworship.org/LeadMe

Lead me to a place of rest.
Lead me to a place of peace.
Lead me to a place of quiet
in your presence, Jesus.

I find my home in you.
I find myself in you.
I find my peace anew
in your presence, Jesus.

Longing to lay down my load.
Longing to lay down my shame.
Longing to lay down my striving
in your presence, Jesus.

Sam Hargreaves

Chapter 13
Restless Devices

Buzzzz. Ping. Alert. Red dot. "Look at this!" "Pay attention to me!" "You're missing something important!"

The demanding nature of our technology - phones, tablets, laptops, smart-watches and more - amplifies exponentially the distraction we spoke of in the previous chapters. Sociologist Felicia Wu Song says of our "restless devices":

> "While we are so grateful and even love so much of what we get from our digital technologies, we often feel frustrated, harassed, and exhausted by them. And we don't know what to do about it."[1]

Never before in history have humans been bombarded with 24 / 7 / 365 incessant calls on their attention. With our phones in our pockets and by our bedsides, we can literally end up with no "down time" at all - the news, social media, work email and

---

1   Felicia Wu Song, *Restless Devices*, (InterVarsity Press, 2021) page 4.

a hundred other distractions clamour at us every moment. Even times previously considered set apart - church services, prayer times, date nights, family meals, toilet breaks - get interrupted. The natural "margin" previously created by waiting for a bus, or in a supermarket queue, or taking a coffee break is now eliminated by the urge to check, scroll, respond.

Is it any wonder that we struggle to rest? We were not created to be "on call" at all times. Jesus himself modelled the radical alternative to this, regularly switching off from the demands of the crowds and even his disciples to be alone with his Father. In Luke 5 for example, he has healed a man with leprosy, and he asks him not to tell anyone. But Luke records:

> "Yet the news about him spread all the more, so that crowds of people came to hear him and to be healed of their sicknesses. But Jesus often withdrew to lonely places and prayed." (Luke 5:15-16)

Jesus was aware of the importance of time where nothing was being demanded of him. He intentionally removed himself from situations where people were asking things of him (even good things, such as healing), and allowed his soul to be restored in the quiet. If Jesus had had a smartphone, do you think he would have taken it with him to the lonely places? Somehow I doubt it...

Phones and technology offer us many benefits. We saw during the COVID-19 pandemic the blessings of being able to meet online when buildings were closed. The group chat for our local street proved a lifeline of information, encouragement and community. The ability to video call with friends and grandparents across the country and the world continues to be of great value. It's likely that you could list many other ways in which your devices are genuinely useful. I would go as far as to say that technological development can be seen as a good gift from God.

The question with all of God's good gifts is: will we use them in ways which honour God, and promote flourishing for ourselves and our world? Will the gift of gold be used as a beautiful offering of worship, or will we turn that gold into an idol and bow down and worship the gift, rather than the giver?

Often, our phones control us, when we should control our phones. Try an experiment: turn your phone off and put it on a shelf (if you have people who are dependent on you, warn them in advance and perhaps give them an alternative way of contacting you). How long can you leave that phone before your fingers get itchy? I have to confess, I do not find this easy.

In the previous chapter we talked about the importance of pausing. Pausing the clamour of our phones is not only important: it's far more achievable than we might think. Here are some ways to tame your device that you can try:

App purge. Do a little inventory: does this app add to my thriving? For example, I've deleted almost all the games I had on my phone, because I found them to be Counterfeit Rest rather than adding any benefit to my life. I also wear an analogue watch, so I don't look at my phone to check the time and then get distracted by something on the screen.

Separate work from personal. In some jobs it is ideal to have a work phone which you can switch off when you're not doing your work hours. I've never had email on my personal phone, because email is 95% work for me. Limiting email to my computer means I only check it when I sit down to work; it's not constantly interrupting me during evenings, meals and days off.

Adjust the alert settings. You don't need every app to send you an alert for everything it deems important. *You* should decide what's important. Personally, I limit alerts to phonecalls, texts and WhatsApp messages only. Similarly to the email hack, it means I only look at Facebook and other apps when I intentionally open them.

Greyscale mode. Most smartphones have the option to let you switch from colour to greyscale mode. All the functionality remains, but it looks a lot more dull and less exciting for your brain, and many people find this reduces the urge to check their phone.

Use weekends, retreats and holidays to switch off. Most of us have jobs and social lives which mean we can't be complete luddites every day. However, there are times when it can be possible to literally put your devices in a drawer for a day or more. Set "out of office" messages, give loved ones alternative ways to contact you, and then enjoy the pleasures of nature, physical books, face-to-face conversations, music played on vinyl and the sheer sound of silence.

Chapter 14
Counter-Liturgies

We've discussed the distracting nature of technology, but unfortunately the influence of our devices goes further. The truth is that it's no accident that our phones hook us in. They are intentionally designed by tech companies to distract us. John Mark Comer quotes the first president of Facebook, Sean Parker, as saying:

> "The thought process that went into building these applications, Facebook being the first of them… was all about 'how can we consume as much of your time and conscious attention as possible?'"[1]

Comer goes on to quote the poet Mary Oliver's phrase "Attention is the beginning of devotion", and reflects:

> "Worship and joy start with the capacity to turn our minds' attention toward the God who is always with us in the now

---

1   Sean Parker quoted in *The Ruthless Elimination of Hurry*, (Hodder & Stoughton, 2019) page 38.

[...] when we uncritically hurry our way through our digital terrain, we make the devil's job relatively easy."[2]

When we give large proportions of our mental attention to the demands of our screens they quietly and insidiously become objects of devotion. As we idolise them, they begin to shape us in return. As William Blake put it, "They become like what they behold!"[3]

Felicia Wu Song points out that social media is a kind of "secular liturgy".[4] We have our repeated "ritual" actions of checking, posting, responding; appeasing the demanding idol in our pockets.

Your church's gathered worship will be structured around some sort of liturgy, whether that be the formal, spoken ritual of a traditional church or the informal, sung, free flowing liturgy of a contemporary church. These repeated patterns and habits of songs, prayers, and actions reveal to us, bit by bit, what abundant life in Jesus looks like. These worship practices help form us, over time, into the likeness of Christ.

The digital world with its "secular liturgy" also gives us its own sense of the "good life" and over time, the more we engage with it, the more we are formed into the image that it presents to us. Everything about digital media is intentionally designed to *form* you in a certain way. Feel frustrated that you have to

---

2   John Mark Comer, *The Ruthless Elimination of Hurry*, (Hodder & Stoughton, 2019) page 53.

3   William Blake, *Jerusalem, The Emanation of the Giant Albion*, plate 65:79.

4   Felicia Wu Song, *Restless Devices*, (InterVarsity Press, 2021) page 134, drawing on the work of philosopher James KA Smith.

keep scrolling down to find the Facebook posts that interest you? That's Facebook's way of keeping your attention. Get anxious with the tone of online news? That's how the news people keep you reading their updates. Get angry at toxic Twitter discussions? That's how they keep you tweeting. Feel insecure when you see perfect Instagram posts? That's what makes you go out and buy the products the influencers are touting. And so on.

The image that digital media forms in us is often frustrated, anxious, angry and insecure. It is the exact opposite of the rest, peace, love and security that Jesus offers.

Wu Song suggests that what we need, rather than simply throwing our phones away, are "counter-liturgies"; repeated actions and practices which replace the habits our phones have taught us.[5] These can be found in the formal setting of gathered worship, but they ought also to be part of our daily lives.

Some examples of counter-liturgies which have helped us as a family include:

Morning routine. I used to wake up and immediately check my phone. I had some excuse that I was using it as an alarm clock, but inevitably I'd then see any alerts, and it was only a click away to start looking at Facebook, the news or being drawn into work issues on WhatsApp. This then snowballed into anxiety, stress or, at the very least, distraction. Any attempts to pray or start the day with God were hi-jacked.

---

5 Felicia Wu Song, *Restless Devices*, (InterVarsity Press, 2021) pages 137-149.

Now instead we put our phones "to bed" downstairs at 9pm. We bought cheap alarm clocks, and my morning liturgy begins with spending some quiet time with God. It may take a few days, but it isn't long before this new, restful, worshipful way of beginning the day becomes something you don't want to miss.

Mealtimes. Eating as a family around the table feels like a counter-cultural thing to do in our day. And making mealtimes a phone-free zone acts as a counter-liturgy to the prevailing tide of screens at the table. What has surprised us is that we, the adults, are the main transgressors in this area - we can often find an excuse to pull out our phones and google something, or just answer this message... If we can resist, the resulting conversations, giggles and sense of being present to one another are precious and formative gifts for our family.

What are we listening to? I - Sam - used to have my ear-buds on all the time, listening to podcasts, music and the radio. I haven't cut this out entirely, but I am being more intentional about having times when I don't plug myself in. In fact, this was another reason I stopped taking my phone to bed - I used to listen to something to help me sleep. However, having stopped that habit I now think I sleep better without the chatter in my ears. Similarly, I'm seeing the benefit of doing the washing up and other mundane tasks with nothing to distract me: I can focus on that task, think through any emotions or issues I am facing, and give space for God to speak.

Night time. Not taking our phones to bed also meant re-thinking our nighttime liturgy. Sara writes a couple of lines in a 5-year diary and looks back at what she was doing in previous years (this is a good alternative to posting and scrolling on Facebook). Sam pauses to pray an *examen* prayer,[6] then we both read a few pages of paper books before turning in. Being present to God, ourselves and one another last thing at night is forming us into healthier people.

Reflect:

Where do you feel digital devices are forming you in ways you don't feel are healthy? Is it to do with Instagram, online news, YouTube binges, toxic debates, indecent images, celebrity gossip… or something else? What are some counter-liturgies you could put in place to re-centre your attention back on God?

---

6 See Chapter 38.

Chapter 15
Slowing Down

When we were first married, Sara and I used to go and visit my grandparents. The pace of life in their house seemed so different to the world around us. There was very little rushing, stressing, hurrying. Afternoons stretched out before us with no particular agenda. There was gentle conversation, cups of tea and quite a bit of silence. It was initially unsettling; we'd often check our watches just to see that, yes, only three minutes had passed in what seemed like an hour. But over time, and more so now that they are no longer with us, we came to treasure those slow, soul-restoring days.

We've talked about rests in music, but music also has *tempo*. That's the speed the piece is played at, measured in Beats Per Minute (BPM). The tempo of most of our lives is remarkably high, as we move quickly from one thing to the next. Technology and advertisers promise that their products will help us do things faster, with increased pace and efficiency.

Interestingly, BPM is also how we measure our heart rate. Generally speaking, the fitter and more relaxed we are, the lower our resting heart rate is, and the slower our breathing. But ill health, stress and mindless living increases our BPM and causes us to take shallower, faster breaths.

Reflect:

Pause for a moment and sense your own body - how fast does your heart seem to be going? How slowly and deeply are you breathing? Do these things indicate something about the pace of your life?

Slow spirituality

A few years ago we wrote an Advent resource called *Worship in the Waiting*. We explored the idea that Jesus was slow, not hurried. Present, not rushed. Patient, not anxious. And we loved reflecting on this verse:

> "The Lord is not slow in keeping his promise, as some understand slowness. Instead he is patient with you". (2 Pet 3:9)

Makoto Fujimura is an internationally renowned visual artist who specialises in what has been called "slow art", based on his training in the Japanese tradition of *Nihonga*.[1] This uses precious materials, painstakingly mixed and prepared by hand. Each layer may take weeks to dry, and a painting might include up to 60

---

1   Explore further in Makoto Fujimura, *Art + Faith*, (Yale University Press, 2021) and https://makotofujimura.com

layers - can you imagine creating work at that kind of pace? He encourages viewers to look at each work for at least 10-15 minutes, slowly allowing the layers to be revealed to their eyes. New York Times critic David Brooks called his work "a small rebellion against the quickening of time."[2]

As a Christian, Fujimura sees slowing down as an opportunity to enter into a more godly pace of life, to begin to see the world through God's eyes. Sam had the privilege of interviewing him for a podcast, and Makoto shared this:

> "I have spoken to so many worship leaders, a lot of them very successful, major churches, megachurches, leading, very famous in that sense. And I ask them 'How are you doing creatively? I know you are doing well in your job... but how are you doing creatively?' and 90% tell me [whispers] 'I'm not doing very well.' And as an artist I can already sense that, there's a level of burnout, there's a level of expectation [...] what's difficult is our churches don't allow us to slow down, and reflect, and to behold."[3]

Slow down. Reflect. Behold.

You may or may not be a worship leader, or consider yourself an artist or creative. But all of us need this opportunity - to slow down, reflect and behold the world around us.

Our culture values rush and hurry, prizing efficiency over patience,

2   David Brooks, "Longing for an Internet Cleanse", *New York Times*, 3/28/19.

3   *Resound Worship Songwriting Podcast*, episode 100, resoundworship.org/podcast

but these things do not allow us the pauses and rests we need. We can learn from "slow art" to practise "slow spirituality".

Ideas to try:

Live counter-culturally by trying some of the following:

- walk to places instead of driving;
- grow something from seed, submitting yourself to nature's schedule;
- choose the longer line in the check-out queue;
- cook something from scratch rather than heating a ready meal or getting a takeaway;
- write a physical letter or a card to someone using your handwriting, not a device;
- spend time with a toddler or older person who takes life at a slower pace;
- avoid multi-tasking, instead mono-task, giving what you are doing your full attention (even if it appears boring!).

With each of these ideas, use the slower pace to try to be fully aware of what you are doing, what you are sensing with your sight, touch, taste, smell and hearing, and how you are feeling on the inside.

Pray:

Make use of the confession prayer on the next page.[4]

---

4   From *Worship in the Waiting: Church Service Pack*, engageworship.org/waiting

Jesus, Prince of Peace,
teach us to walk in your rhythms of grace.

Holy God, forgive our impatience with everyday life.
We rush around, irritated at delays,
frustrated with things and people
which do not move at the pace we would like.
Jesus, Prince of Peace,
teach us to walk in your rhythms of grace.

Holy God, forgive our impatience
with answers to prayer.
Sometimes we treat you like a vending machine,
or assume to know your will and your best for us.
Help us to trust your timing and your kindness.
Jesus, Prince of Peace,
teach us to walk in your rhythms of grace.

Holy God, forgive our impatience
with your coming again.
You are not slow, you are patient,
and you long for all to come to you willingly.
May we live in holy anticipation of your return.
Jesus, Prince of Peace,
teach us to walk in your rhythms of grace.

Thank you that you are gracious and compassionate,
slow to anger and rich in love.
You are patient with our mistakes and forgive our sins.
We receive your peace afresh today.
Jesus, Prince of Peace,
teach us to walk in your rhythms of grace. Amen.

Chapter 16
Control and Azalea

One of the reasons we don't have healthy rhythms of rest can be that we think we're in control - of our lives, and particularly of other people. Our colleague Timo shared with us:

> "Do you ever get that rush of excitement when you're multitasking and you feel like you are actually extending your capabilities and natural limits? You're in a meeting but you're also replying to a WhatsApp message whilst secretly doing your back exercises. I confess that I feel a bit god-like when I do that!"

There are times when it seems that our multitude of plates are spinning quite nicely, and we feel no need to stop them. Then something comes along to disrupt that - a crisis, a pandemic, another human being - and suddenly we realise that the idea of control was an illusion. The plates start to crash all around us.

I - Sam - lead a Bible study on a Wednesday night for women who are in various stages of exiting domestic and international sex trafficking. Many are also involved in drug addiction and have challenges around homelessness. It is part of a wonderful organisation called Azalea in our home town of Luton.[1]

What I learn from leading that Bible study each week is this: I cannot control this situation! I can plan. I can put in boundaries and employ safeguarding policies. But I can't control the level with which the women engage with the songs, prayers and discussions, and I certainly can't control what they do when they leave the building at 7pm.

Often I want to say: "Leave him! Stop doing that! Move out of that squat! Get your life together!" But transformation for these women does not look like that: it's a much longer, slower journey of discovering the riches of who they are in Christ, realising that they have meaningful choices and opportunities, that there is grace and mercy for every time they slip and regress. Allowing decades of trauma to be replaced by these eternal truths is a life's work, and it may not be complete until Resurrection Day. And so walking with them, introducing them to Jesus and life in abundance can never be an exercise in control, but in yielding them to Jesus.

Leading worship for these women is also a great immersion into letting go of control. Today, worship leaders tend to choose all the songs - in fact, they can get quite upset if a congregation member or even a pastor suggests something they might play! But at Azalea it's different. We have a folder with about 20 of

---

1 azalea.org.uk

our favourite songs in it. It's a mix of old hymns, modern songs, and a few written within our community. Rather than plan each week's song set, I arrive and say "Right, what are we singing today, ladies?" Everyone gets to choose. If you're new, you might just pick based on a title that jumps out to you. Regulars have their favourites - we seem to sing Waymaker and Amazing Grace every week.

Once we've sung a song, everyone affirms the choice. "That was a good one, Gloria!" "Great choice, Janice!" It's a small thing, but in a world that tries to control them and rid them of meaningful decisions, it affirms that each woman has choices she can make.

While they are learning this, I'm learning to give up control. I'm allowing them to be themselves, giving them options, pointing towards Jesus, and trusting that the Holy Spirit will do the rest.

The truth is, Azalea isn't really so different to normal life and normal church. Our reluctance to pause and rest can often be rooted in our desperate attempts to control people and situations. We feel that if we just keep working, everything will go as we intend. But at the end of the day, you can't control anyone else - your church congregation, your colleagues, your family, your neighbours (unless you're manipulating or abusing them). The Kingdom of God comes slowly, mysteriously, and we need patience and trust to see it emerge.

Walking in rhythms of rest means relinquishing control. Times of rest give us the opportunity to say: I've done enough. I will lay down my tools. I will entrust that situation to Jesus. I will yield these people to God.

Reflect:

If you struggle with healthy rhythms of rest, to what extent might that be to do with control issues in your heart? Are there people you want to influence or situations you want to manipulate to the degree that you can't take a break?

Pray:

Clench your fists tightly, imagining those people and situations held in your hands. Name them before God. Then slowly release your fists, choosing to release control of these things to God. Receive his peace.

Chapter 17
Saying No - the Parable of the Curtains

Recently, at the Bible study I mentioned in the last chapter, my wonderful, godly friend and co-leader Carmel started telling a story about a strange couple who turned up uninvited at her door. They knew her by name and seemed grateful that she still lived in the same house, but she had to admit that she had no idea who they were. The older lady introduced herself and said "Years ago, I had some curtains that needed taking up, and you did the sewing for me. Well, now my daughter here has these new curtains, and we want you to do the same for her."

Around the table at the Bible study we laughed alongside Carmel at the audacity of this request, and commiserated with her as she described how, in her surprised and bemused state, she not only invited these strange women into her house, but also agreed to do the work for them!

Later on, our passage for the evening was Matthew 11:28-30, "Come to me all you heavy laden... for my yoke is easy and my burden is light". We talked about burdens people were carrying, in society and in our own lives, and how Jesus promises to bear our burdens. At this point, Carmel joked, "Do you think Jesus will take the burden of my curtains from me?" and we all laughed again.

But then one of the other leaders, Anthea, surprised us with a thought: "Carmel, maybe Jesus will bear your burdens, by giving you the courage to call those people up and telling them that, no, sorry, you can't do their curtains after all." Mic drop. None of us had thought of it like that.

Maybe this is a picture of how so many of us live. We don't like saying "no" to people. We want to come across as friendly, hardworking and helpful. There are always lots of invitations to do things in the world - join clubs, serve on boards, do chores or errands for people, volunteer in church activities... and often when we take on a new thing, rather than replace an existing commitment, we add that latest activity onto our already toppling pile.

All this adds up to the point where we feel overwhelmed, overbusy and overburdened. Someone will tell us that Jesus wants to bear our load, and we imagine him swooping down on a chariot to lift our responsibilities and commitments off our shoulders.

But perhaps, like with Carmel and her curtains, Jesus wants to do a deeper work.

He wants to free us from our fear of saying "no"; release us to balance our own diaries, workload and commitments. He wants us to see that our worth is not measured by the amount of things we do for other people or the amount of activity and ministry we can generate.

We need to know that our value is rooted in being a child of God - eternally loved, accepted and delighted in. The more secure we are in this knowledge, the more we will be able to soberly assess the requests people make of us. When we build our lives on that foundation, we'll be able to set our priorities with God, and then kindly but confidently say "no" to the things that aren't ours to take on; the burdens that aren't ours to carry.

Does that change the way you view this verse?

"For my yoke is easy and my burden is light." (Matt 11:30)

The idea of a "yoke" is a metaphor drawn from the wooden crossbar carried across the shoulders of an ox. Walter Brueggemann suggests it may have referred to the tax system of the Roman empire, or to "the endless requirements of an over-coded religious system that required endless attentiveness."[1] As well as political and religious burdens, today we might think of all the heavy expectations we carry in society, in trying to fit in with our colleagues, friends and families. It's the rucksack of pressures, demands and assumptions on our backs. We all carry such a yoke, and left unchecked it gets heavier and more ill-fitting by the day.

---

1   Walter Brueggemann, *Sabbath As Resistance*, (Westminster John Knox Press, 2014) page 11.

Reflect:

Note down - what are the burdens, expectations and pressures that you are carrying?

In contrast, Jesus' yoke fits you perfectly. His expectations of you don't go beyond what you can manage. He desires that you live freely, not weighed down by other people's expectations and demands. As the Message version puts it: "Keep company with me and you'll learn to live freely and lightly."

Pray:

Bring your burdens to Jesus. Ask him to show you the things he is calling you to carry, and the things of which you should let go. You may want to listen to the song *The Gospel is Rest* by Elias Dummer; its lyrics sum up these sentiments perfectly.[2]

---

2   engageworship.org/redirect/GospelRest

Chapter 18
Resisting the Powers

Some workplaces, cultures and contexts are hard-wired for stress, hurry and overwork. I was chatting with a friend and we agreed that just as institutional racism, sexism and ageism exist insidiously in many places, institutional workaholism is just as present. It may not be on the official job descriptions or written into the published values of the organisation, but inhuman expectations, coercion and a fundamental resistance to rest are all too often baked-into work cultures. This is no better - and it's often worse - in Christian contexts.

We've worked for churches where every employee answered the question "how are you?" with an almost inevitable "busy" or "tired". We wore that like a badge of honour. We were doing Kingdom work! We were changing the world and reaching new people. We could rest when we were old, or dead. I've joked with friends that some Christians seem to have taken inspiration from that line in the song *Waymaker* a little too personally: "You never stop, you never stop working..."

When we act like this we play directly into our enemy's hands. We anxiously fear that the world will fall apart if we don't keep working. We start to resent other people who don't do as much. And our bodies and souls begin to suffer and die under the pressure of this kind of unceasing toil. We ignore the invitation of God to rest and instead fall for the world, the flesh and the Devil's culture of workaholism.

Old Testament scholar Walter Brueggemann points to Egypt as the archetype of the restless, anxious, coercive culture.[1] They poured increasingly burdensome expectations on the Israelite slaves: make more bricks! Make bricks without straw! When Israel escapes in the Exodus, they are being liberated from inhuman workloads. But it will be all too easy for them to revert back to old bondage, or even to become oppressors themselves.

In Exodus 20, the reason given for Sabbath is that God rested in Creation. But in Deuteronomy 5, when the Ten Commandments are re-stated, the commentary is different:

> "On it you shall not do any work, neither you, nor your son or daughter, nor your male or female servant, nor your ox, your donkey or any of your animals, nor any foreigner residing in your towns, so that your male and female servants may rest, as you do. *Remember that you were slaves in Egypt and that the Lord your God brought you out of there with a mighty hand and an outstretched arm.*" (Deut 5:14-15, emphasis added)

---

1   Walter Brueggemann, *Sabbath As Resistance*, (Westminster John Knox Press, 2014) Chapter 3.

Here, Sabbath becomes a reminder that they have been liberated from oppressive work. It resists the powers that would keep them enslaved to anxious, dehumanising toil. And importantly, it demands not only that they rest, but that their children, animals, servants and any foreigners get to rest too.

This points to our need for a "Sabbath economy" - a culture that embodies the depth of God's vision for Sabbath with an "equitable distribution of resources".[2] If people do not have their basic physical needs met, they will not be able to enter into the rest they are due. If they are on dehumanising zero-hours contracts or forced to work every day of the week, our culture is treating them with the same coercive attitude as Pharaoh of old.

Rest is not supposed to be a privilege for the wealthy or powerful few. When we rest, we need to make sure that others can rest too. This means pro-actively changing cultures of workaholism and unpicking structures of dehumanising toil. For those of us in any position of privilege, leadership or influence, this will mean making some hard decisions.

Reflect:

Are there situations you have influence over - people you lead, ways you use your money, employment contracts etc. - where your decisions might be holding people back from entering in to God's Sabbath economy? How can the way you live free other people to also enter into rest?

---

2   Norman Wirzba, cited in Ruth Haley Barton, *Embracing Rhythms of Work and Rest*, (InterVarsity Press 2022) pages 33-34.

Start with your heart

These questions have practical, external implications. However, for many of us the root causes are less to do with institutional factors and more to do with our heart attitudes. Ask yourself: if I overwork, why is that? We can often blame the expectations of others, or the cultures we are part of. But the reality is that most of us have far more choice than we will admit. Choices about how we organise our diaries; about what we say yes and no to; about how many hours we work.

Don Tassone wrote a blog about burnout in which he intended to expose institutional failures. He gathered statistics on how companies treated their employees and mistreated their workforce. But then he had a revelation:

> "I was burned out. But why? It's tempting to blame my company or the nature of the type of work I chose to do [...] [But] If I'm honest with myself, my burnout was largely self-inflicted."[3]

He goes on to list 5 things he would do differently if he could have his working life again: take ownership; be clear about what's most important; start my day with 10 minutes of quiet; take care of myself; be more humble.

Pray

Ask God to show you what it would look like to resist workaholism in your own heart and life.

---

3   Don Tassone, *Confessions Of A Workaholic,* medium.com

Chapter 19
Badges and Solitude

I like badges. Pin badges, metal badges, sew-on badges, the lot. They can be colourful and decorative, or have funny slogans like "To err is human, to arr is pirate" or "If you can read this you're too close." I still have my Deputy Head Boy badge from when I was at school - which is weird because a) *Deputy* Head Boy isn't really that special and b) I can't remember ever actually doing anything in that role. But I keep it because somehow I'm proud of it. It is literally a *badge of honour*.

People wear badges to express something of their identity. It might have the name of a band they like, a political slogan or a sports team they support. Others wear badges connected to their role or their job: a work ID lanyard, a "Happy to Help" till operator badge, military service medals, a sign on our desk or our door.

There are badges on our clothes in the form of labels, and on our car emblems, and the logos on our phones. For some people it's important to be seen in the right outfit, driving the right car or carrying the right gadget.

Scouts and Guides have "merit" badges for skills they've acquired or achievements they've earned. For the rest of us, we have to rely on dropping our achievements into conversation (as subtly as possible, of course), or posting about them on social media.

All of this is about *identity*. Through our badges (literal and metaphorical) we project to the world: this is who I am. I am the sum total of these roles / possessions / achievements / opinions / relationships. We even do it with faith, signalling to the world which kind of Christian we are in the form of our theological stance, our favourite worship music, the kind of Bible we read, the conferences and events we go to, and in many other ways.

None of these things are wrong in and of themselves. Exploring, celebrating and expressing our identity is a good thing. However, the question might be: what is the *root* of my identity? Who am I at the deepest level? The badges are all attempts to define ourselves from the outside-in. We're covering ourselves up with achievements and activity and possessions, a bit like Adam and Eve tried to cover their nakedness with fig leaves in Genesis 3 .

But God defines us from the inside-out. Words like "soul", "spirit", "heart" and "inner being" point towards a deeper reality, a secret inner place where God is at work to define us:

> "I pray that out of his glorious riches he may strengthen you with power *through his Spirit* in your *inner being*, so that Christ may dwell *in your hearts* through faith." (Eph 3:16-17, emphasis added)

Solitude is a place where the badges come off. God hasn't primarily given us the gift of solitude because people are annoying or exhausting (although they are), or even as a way of recharging depleted batteries (although it can help with that). Choosing to spend time away from others is a way of slowly taking the badges off. Of allowing myself to be defined not by my activity, what I achieve, what I wear, or how I speak or act.

And this is why I think I struggle with solitude. I get used to hiding behind my busyness, my social interactions and my roles. To walk away from those things, even for an hour, can lead me to wonder "who am I?" Who am I if I'm not achieving things, helping people, expressing my opinions, fulfilling my roles?

Reflect:

How do you feel about the idea of solitude? How comfortable are you to be on your own with God and no other distractions or markers of identity?

This is a challenge, but it is also an opportunity. As I take off my badges and lay them down, one by one, I begin to breathe a little deeper. I realise that although these things may be part of me, they do not ultimately define me. Some of them might be unhealthy. Others might be good, but may have taken too much prominence in my life.

The more I lay these identity badges down, the more I create space for God to show me who I really am.

> "It's in Christ that we find out who we are and what we are living for. Long before we first heard of Christ and got

our hopes up, he had his eye on us, had designs on us for glorious living" (Eph 1:11-12 MSG)

It may feel scary to lay down your badges, but doing this with God is actually the safest place to do it. Much better to loosen your grip on these outer forms of identity within the security of God's embrace, rather than be forced to give them up when you lose a job, a relationship breaks down or illness strikes. All our outer badges can be taken away, but being rooted in God is a firm foundation.

Reflect:

Think about the badges you wear - your roles, achievements, possessions, relationships and more. Note down the ways you define your identity and express that to others.

Then take some time laying those things down before God. Allow him to speak to you about those things.

Finally, spend some time receiving from God. Know him defining you: you are his child, his friend, his beloved. You are in Christ. Your identity is secure in him.

Chapter 20
Finding Rhythms

In this part of the book, we've looked at various ways you can explore rhythms of rest. Ways you can pause, resisting the pressures and busyness of our culture, choosing to lay something down for a moment in order to receive the gift of rest Jesus holds out to you. Before we move on, let's get practical about how you can include these pauses as rhythms in your life.

If you were to write down the famous rhythm part for Queen's *We Will Rock You*, it would look like two beats stomping with your feet, one clapping your hands, and one rest. That rest might not feel important, but just try leaving it out! You will either add another hit on beat four (losing that lovely, anticipatory gap), or you will skip beat four altogether and switch the song from 4/4 time to 3/4, waltz time. Not very rock and roll!

Rests are vital for rhythm. Rhythms are repeated patterns, and God has woven them into the fabric of creation. There are the giant rhythms dictated by our planet's movement around the sun:

the years, the seasons, day turning to night turning to day. There are tides washing in and out, the moon waxing and waning. There are the more intimate rhythms of our heartbeats, our footsteps, our speech patterns. All of these rhythms feature both activity and pause.

Think about the year, for example. It is vital for nature that we have both winter and summer. The ground, the plants and the animals need a season of things dying off, of being still and cold and dormant, in order that they can burst back into life again the next year.

Similarly, our lives need rhythms of activity and pause. We need times of movement, interaction and fruitfulness. But we also need times of stillness, solitude and unproductiveness.

Our planet has its 365 day rhythm of orbiting the sun, and its 24 hour rhythm of rotating in its orbit. Similarly, we need both macro and micro rhythms. Here are some of our experiences; reflect on how the following might apply to you.

Rhythms to reflect on:

Daily. What are your moments of rest each day? Can you create space for solitude, being with God, being present to your surroundings and your emotions? For us, a key moment has become how we spend the early morning: we get up a bit earlier than we used to and take some time with God.[1] For you, mornings might not be possible. How about using your lunch

---

1 Chapter 29 goes deeper into re-thinking "quiet times".

break wisely, reconsidering your evening schedule, taking a walk mid-afternoon, or some other approach?

Weekly. Consider the rhythm of your week when it comes to work and rest. Do you work your set hours, or more? Is there time set aside for chores, volunteering and other draining activities, and then also time for genuine rest and renewal? For us, this has included some practical considerations around weekends: our work computers and email get switched off on a Friday evening. We aim to get chores done on a Saturday so that Saturday evening and Sunday become genuine Sabbath.[2] And if we *have* to do paid work on weekends, we aim to take Time Off In Lieu the following week to compensate. What would this need to look like for you?

Termly or monthly. This depends a bit on how you organise yourself: some people (especially those with kids or in education) think about "term time". Others may plan based on each month. But either way, do you have time for good rest (perhaps a half-day, a day, or even an overnight) in these periods for attending to your soul's needs?

Yearly. Where does rest feature in your year? Do you make sure to take all your vacation time? We have made it a priority to get away for a good chunk of time in the summer holidays, and also try to spend a night or two away from home as a family in the other school breaks (when we're in our house, there are always chores and devices to distract us!). We also look to go on

---

2   See Chapter 28 for more practical ideas around structuring a Sabbath.

individual spiritual retreats once a year.[3] What does this yearly rhythm need to look like for you, in order that you get some truly restorative time?

Over decades. It might sound strange to think of your life in periods of more than a year - it is hard to get our heads around such long stretches of time. But in Leviticus 25 God initiates two meta-seasons: a Sabbath on every seventh year when "the land is to have a year of rest" (verse 5), and a Jubilee every 50 years. In this year people were to return to their home towns, debts were to be cancelled, property returned and slaves freed. This may be an encouragement to view our own lives in "seasons". Think back over your life. If you have worked for many years, do you need a "fallow" time? It may be possible to take a Sabbatical, or some unpaid leave, or to change jobs and do something very different. What season is your life coming into, and where does rest feature in that?[4]

---

3   See Chapter 30 for more on retreats.

4   Ruth Haley Barton has four excellent chapters on Sabbatical in *Embracing Rhythms of Work and Rest*, (InterVarsity Press, 2022).

Part Three:
a restful life

Chapter 21
Managing the Void

When we've pressed the pause-button on our work, our striving and our busyness, we may be left with an echoing quiet and a question: "what now?" How do we rest in godly ways? Is there a Christian way of resting? This conundrum reminds me of Jesus' warning about the eight impure spirits returning to a tidied up house from Matthew 12:43-45, or the old adage "nature abhors a vacuum". If there is space, something will fill it, so *we* need to decide what that something is.

We've all had the experience of chasing a nap (or some other restful activity) during a weekend, only for it to be pushed further and further forward by chores we need to get done and other mysterious time-fillers, until it's suddenly Monday morning and the chance of a nap has been missed for another week.

Or we've started a work-day with the intention of going for a run once we've finished a particular task. Except inevitably, the job is never done and the run never happens. *Parkinson's Law* wryly observes that "work expands so as to fill the time available for its completion."

I have a friend who has the best job title ever, evoking imagery of sci-fi, superheroes or perhaps something out of a Dr Who storyline. She's our local council's *Void Manager*. In boring old reality it has nothing to do with the space-time continuum, and everything to do with what the council does with its housing in between tenants.

But when it comes to rest, we all need to be our own Void Managers. We need to be wise in how we manage the void that opens up when we take seriously the call to cease our work.

Reflect:

Let's do an exercise for a moment. Think about what you would consider your most recent day-off from work (remember that work doesn't automatically mean paid employment; perhaps you're a stay-at-home parent, an unemployed person working hard with job applications or physical rehabilitation, or you might be a retired person volunteering, and so on).

On the next page you will find a chart. Along the vertical time, jot down what you got up to during your day-off. Next, in the right hand column, grade how restful your activities were, with 0 being not restful at all and 5 being totally restful and soul-refreshing.

activities: *grade:*

Morning △

_____   _____

_____   _____

_____   _____

_____   _____

_____   _____

_____   _____

_____   _____

_____   _____

_____   _____

_____   _____

_____   _____

Bed time ▽ _____   _____

Now, very few of us have days with no stress whatsoever, so don't beat yourself up if up until now your "rest" has been less than soul-nourishing. What matters is that you reflect on your practice and think about what works and doesn't work for you.

As I reflect in this way, I can identify several things I habitually do because I think they should be restful, but that actually involve both striving and stress. You may have discovered this for yourself too. My list includes, but is not limited to: scrolling through social media, going shopping, cooking a Sunday roast on an actual Sunday after church, leading worship with a large band and a big PA, going to social events that go on past 9pm, and so on. These might count as, what we called in Chapter Five, Counterfeit Rest.

My examples may not be things you find stressful, so it's important to keep in mind that one person's rest is another person's chore. Our 12-year old son had the time of his life getting to mow the lawn on the farm back in Sweden, because it involved using the ride-on lawn mower, whereas this is one of my least favourite chores. This is why it's not helpful to tell anyone exactly what they must do to nourish their souls.

For the professional chef, cooking at home is just more work, whereas for the accountant it might be a multi-sensory, joy-filled hobby. To the stay-at-home parent, hanging out with more children may make them want to pull their hair out, whereas for those with no small kids a chat with a 3-year old might be like springtime to a wintry soul.

So please, when you consider how to "manage your void", don't try to be like someone else. Test out some of the things we're about to suggest and you might be surprised to discover new things that give you rest and joy. You might find that the rest you seek and the lightness of spirit you long for is closer and simpler than you think.

Reflect

Spend some time with the quote on the next page from Wayne Muller.[1] Allow it to speak to your soul and lead you into prayer.

---

1   Wayne Muller, *Sabbath*, (Bantam, 2000) pages 126-127.

"The antidote to craving is rest; we quench our thirst with Sabbath tranquillity. We invite a time in which we can taste what we have been given, take delight in what we already have, and see that it is good. We focus less on our lack, and more on our abundance. As we do so, our thirst and hunger for more than we need begins to fall away. In quiet stillness we can identify our genuine needs with more precision, and separate them more easily from our mindless wants and desires."

Wayne Muller, Sabbath

Chapter 22
Rest in Silence

I - Sara - went on my first ever silent retreat last year. For some reason I hadn't quite clocked that the retreat I had booked was a silent one - I'd just searched around online until I found a retreat in the area and on the days that suited me. I had unknowingly set myself up for quite a surprise.

After making myself comfortable in my assigned room, the dinner bell rang and I shuffled along to the dining hall, steeling myself for the encounter with the rest of the retreat group. I ended up seated by a table with three or four other guests, and over the meal I learned a lot about them: one was Finnish - and I mentally prepared myself to go through the Scandinavian bonding chat that always happens when I meet someone like me. Another woman almost immediately bared her soul and shared how much she struggled with being single - and I felt sadness and compassion with her, a bit of guilt for having just spoken about my wonderful husband, slight concern that this lady would fill all the available emotional space this retreat and had another dose of guilt for even having those thoughts! A man at our table was a Methodist minister getting ready for the Advent season - and I made a mental note to let him know about the amazing new Advent resource we had just published.

Before I had time to get to the next stage in the conversation, however, Sister Mary stood up to welcome us. She talked us through the program of the retreat, gave us some housekeeping notices and finished with this bombshell:

> "I hope you enjoyed the meal and the conversations you've shared. Because from now on, *we will ask you to keep the silence*. During meal times, there is no need to sit with each other or wait for each other to finish, as we won't be conversing."

The sense of relief I felt in that moment was palpable. I'd say the cost of the retreat was worth it for that moment alone. The fact that I wouldn't have to have the same repeated conversation about what it is to be Scandinavian in Britain, that I didn't have to carry all those emotions about the other people in the room, that there was no space for that self-promotion we often feel we *ought* to engage with - it really felt like burdens lifting from my shoulders.

I had been given the gift of silence.

Reflect:

How do you feel about silence? Does it feel like a gift to you or are you anxious at the very thought of it? What do you fear in the silence? Perhaps take a moment to reflect or journal now.

The wise writer of Ecclesiastes says:

> "Do not be quick with your mouth,
>   do not be hasty in your heart
>   to utter anything before God.
> God is in heaven
>   and you are on earth,
>   so let your words be few." (Ecc 5:2)

Most of us have not been formed into a spirituality of few words. The opposite is more likely true. In our Western society, words are everywhere; on screens, in books, on billboards, on signs to obey and forms to fill in. On the radio, the television, on YouTube and social media - people are constantly talking at us.

Church doesn't seem that different: whether pre-written or improvised, worship is full of words; in songs, liturgies and interaction. Thinking back to how I learned to pray as a young person, there was definitely a scatter-gun approach modelled: just rattle off as many words as possible, sandwiched between "just really" and "Father God", and some might hit the mark. Similarly, we taught our toddlers the old song: "Prayer is like a telephone, for us to talk to Jesus…"

Praise God, that through Jesus he receives our awkward phrases and simple sentences. And I think he loves to hear from us.

But there is more to being with God. Or, I suppose, there is less. Practising silence before God is a way of practising rest as worship. Pause from forming sentences, cease the search for the best words, stop the striving to sound impressive. Relax into a way of praying that just involves placing yourself before God and letting your words be few. Like our image from Chapter 1 of sitting next to a sleepy toddler on a sofa, where the companionship and the pleasure is found in just being present to one another.

Practise being silent before God now:

If it helps you to have a framework, set a timer for how many minutes you have available. See if you can simply *be*, wordless in God's presence. For many of us, one or two anchor words, to pray in time with our breath helps our words at least to be few, if not completely absent. You could whisper or think "Jesus Christ", or another name like "Bread of Life" or "Prince of Peace" which helps you focus. I've taken inspiration from Psalm 46:10 to say the following prayer as I breathe: "Still me. Be known". You will need to find for yourself what words or practices might help you become silent before God.

Chapter 23
Rest in Nature

Some people feel completely at peace worshipping God just about anywhere - they can feel the sacred presence of God in graffiti-covered underpasses or corporate conference rooms. This seems theologically sound to me - by the death and resurrection of Christ and the gift of the Holy Spirit, we can meet with God at any time and in any place. Such grace.

And yet, my own soul is not fully set free to reach for God until I feel a breeze on my cheeks or rest my eyes on the horizon, or at the very least a tree. It's just the way I'm wired. Gary Thomas speaks about nine "spiritual temperaments" in his book *Sacred Pathways*.[1] I found a great sense of relief in reading that he lists "naturalists" first as the pathway the author himself finds most compelling.

Of course, it's a false idea to claim to have only *one* spiritual temperament - I find that I also relate in some way to at least five

---

1   Gary Thomas, *Sacred Pathways*, (Zondervan, 2000).

of Thomas' other pathways. So whether you think of yourself as a "naturalist" or not, nature will have something to offer to you as you consider how your rest can be worship.

Although we can see signs of God's presence everywhere, in the natural environment I feel as though I'm closer to the action somehow. Sure, as I switch on my computer, I can give thanks for the person God made who invented and designed it, for the gift of creativity and the natural resources used to build the machine. But when I touch a tree trunk, I feel several steps closer to God's creative process. This wood, the root system feeding it, the process of photosynthesis keeping it alive come straight from God's mysterious, creative, omniscient heart.

Psalm 19:1 opens in explosive praise: "The heavens declare the glory of God; the skies proclaim the work of his hands", and I agree. As human beings - whether confessing Christians or not - we stand in awe before a snow capped mountain, a fiery sunset or a tall tree. This sensed awe is worship of our Creator, if we know how to direct it.

In an indoor environment, my communion with God is often disrupted by the distraction of the need to perfect something. In my home, there are the scattered shoes of the children to straighten before I can really focus, or the discarded blanket not folded quite right for my liking. Inside a church, the distractions can be overwhelming for me; I wonder why Jesus was made to look so grumpy on the altarpiece, or think that the microphone that the service leader is using is a little too quiet, or I spot cobwebs in a high corner and think about the practicalities of removing them.

Outdoors, my soul can rest in perfection. I couldn't make a better tree if I tried. The wood anemone in Springtime is formed with perfect symmetry. The sunrise is painted in colours unavailable in my watercolour set. "He leads me beside still waters; he restores my soul," we read in Psalm 23:2-3 (NRSV).

There's plenty of scientific research to back up the experience of the psalmist, showing how beneficial nature exposure is to the human soul and mind,[2] including the small matter that just looking at the colour green is relaxing for our eyes.[3] It seems that the need for communion with nature is a built-in human characteristic.

Ideas of how to rest and worship in nature:

Just sit and stare. Find a spot to sit and look at a view in nature. You may want to start by expressing in your heart the awe you experience and the praise arising. Let the words fall away slowly and simply be in God's presence within creation.

Walk in nature. If you have good mobility, carve out some time to walk in the wildest nature that is accessible to you. Rest your eyes on the tree canopy and allow the rhythm of your footsteps to become your meditation.

Rethink your place of prayer. If you normally pray facing a messy room or a wall, could you find a spot in your home with a

---

2   See for example Kirsten Weir, "Nurtured by Nature", engageworship.org/redirect/NurturedByNature

3   Andrew J. Elliot "Color and Psychological Functioning" engageworship.org/redirect/ColourPsychology

view? We live in an urban environment, so I fully appreciate the challenge in this. However, a few years ago, I found a spot in our bedroom where if I angled myself just right, I could rest my eyes on a leafy tree three houses away. This year, as our children have outgrown their toys, I've recently reclaimed the playspace that faces our garden, and my mind is soothed as I see the seasons change outside the window.

Respond:

Take a moment to engage with God in nature now. You can use one of the ideas above, or be with God in creation in some other way that works for you. Receive God's rest as you connect with his world.

Chapter 24
Rest in Joy

I remember the confusion I felt as a teenager as I became totally sold out for Jesus. The discovery of faith for myself coincided with those awkward adolescent years of surly attitudes and sarcasm, and I kept bumping uncomfortably on verses like "Rejoice in the Lord always!" (Phil 4:4). It was something I struggled to obey as I worked out how to become a grown-up.

And as a budding worship leader, I felt joyful while leading and singing songs about how happy I was to belong to Jesus, but then I felt miserable on Monday mornings again. I wrestled with how to match my very real, pretty negative, emotions with my belief that Christians ought to be joyful all the time.

Although I've learned to control the sarcastic outbursts of my youth, I still don't find the "rejoice always" command all that easy. The world is a difficult place and there are plenty of things to feel miserable about. My understanding of faith and worship has broadened too, and I understand that lament is an important part of our response to God and that he's not some kind of tightly wound pageant-mom demanding glittering smiles from us 24/7. He wants to hear how we really feel, and we see in the Psalms that God is okay with us letting rip with our complaints.

As Christians, we can rest assured that we have permission to feel all of the feelings.

But as grown-ups who know about all the bad stuff in the world, don't you just feel like taking a break from misery sometimes? Don't you look at the news headlines occasionally and wish that you could somehow step away from all that?

This, I believe, is another place for rest. Making time for joy is an opportunity for faithful rest. Faithful, in the sense that turning from worry, fear, anger and grief - for however short a moment - to express joy, is an act of trust. It's an act of worship, of declaring who's on the throne and who's in ultimate control. In a world full of misery, our joy can be an almost rebellious presence to those around us. Joy is a place for rest as worship.

Worry and anxiety leave us restless and distracted. The grace of God is that he wants to bear our burdens (Ps 68:19). The call to Sabbath, to cease our work, means also to cease our worries, by leaving our miserable weights there, in God's arms, even if it's just for a day, or even an hour.

When I was researching our family journal *Jesus and Emotions*,[1] I learned a couple of interesting things from the field of psychology.

---

1   engageworship.org/emotions

One was about how differently children and adults experience sadness. A healthy child who has experienced loss won't naturally sink into continuous depression, but will have "breaks" in the grief. They will cry and be angry for a while, and then might have some "time off" building Lego, followed by another moment when they might cry and talk about their loss, but then a friend comes around and they'll play and laugh for a little while, and so on. Their grief moves in waves and they recover more quickly. As adults, we often feel like we're not supposed to laugh in the midst of grief, so we allow the sadness to take over our whole lives and we are flooded by the emotion.

How can we be more like children and live in better balance, allowing for both sadness and joy to be a part of our lives? How can we take breaks in the constant burden of seeing a suffering world all around us?

One way to help us have joy, which the Bible, psychology and a million self-help books all agree on, is to practise gratitude. As children of God, practising gratitude is a fair amount more meaningful than a general "sending good vibes to the universe", but according to research, even a vague sense of thankfulness works as an anchor holding us still in the choppy waters of sadness. Sadness tells us what we have lost, thankfulness tells us what we still have.

The Bible is full of encouragement to give thanks to God, including one of my favourites:

> "Let the peace of Christ rule in your hearts, since as

members of one body you were called to peace. And be
thankful." (Col 3:15)

I find myself accepting the encouragement to *be thankful* more
readily than the command to *rejoice*, perhaps because it feels like
something you can do whether you "feel" it or not. But maybe the
line between thankfulness and joy is a blurry one, because when
you take the time to *really* be thankful - to name all those things
that are answers to yesterday's prayers - a sense of joy begins to
slowly enter your consciousness, like the heat of a roaring fire
slowly defrosting winter-cold toes.

In the next couple of chapters we are going to look at some other
ways in which we might seek out that restful joy we are asked to
engage in. But for now, let's be thankful.

Find a way to practise gratitude

There isn't one right way to give thanks to God, of course, so
you'll need to find a way that fits into your life. This is, however,
a practice that is helpful if it becomes a habit. Because even if
you're not feeling particularly thankful one day, if it's a habitual
part of your life, you may surprise yourself with the change of
perspective you can gain. You could try one of these ideas:

"Count your blessings" at the end of the day. Whether you
engage in an *examen*,[2] or you write a journal entry, or you just
lie down on your bed and close your eyes, could you get into a
habit of listing the things you are thankful for from the day?

---

2   See a full description of this in Chapter 38.

Create a gratitude wall. During the third COVID lockdown in the first few months of 2021, misery levels were high in our family. To give a focus to morning prayer times before another round of homeschooling, we all drew something we were thankful for on little slips of paper and stuck them up on a "gratitude wall" on the inside of a kitchen cupboard door. The build-up of things to be grateful for during those months served as a visual reminder that not everything in our lives was awful.

Habit-stack gratitude. Find something you do every day, for example brush your teeth, make a mid-morning cup of tea or have a shower. See if you can "stack" another habit on top, by taking those moments to mention things to God that you are thankful for. Perhaps you say grace before meals as a family? Rather than saying the same old prayer every day, could you add a moment where everyone says something they are grateful for in that moment. It's one of the easiest prayers for young children to understand and get involved with too.

Pray:

Use the prayer on the next page to choose the joy of Jesus today.[3]

---

3   From *Resurrection People: Church Service Pack*. engageworship.org/resurrection

Jesus, you were filled with joy in the Holy Spirit,
you delighted in the company of laughing children,
you told funny stories and enjoyed a good party.

Forgive us when we confuse holiness
with being humourless.
Sometimes we take ourselves too seriously,
and fail to see the funny side.
We can miss out on childlike joy and wide-eyed
wonder in this world you've made.

Help us to live lightly in your resurrection power,
filled with the joy of our salvation,
grateful for what we have
and content whatever our circumstances.

Help us to rejoice with those who rejoice,
mourn with those who mourn,
giggle uncontrollably
with those who giggle uncontrollably,
and be bringers of your good,
happy news to the world.
Amen.

Chapter 25
Rest in Play

I - Sam - was playing with our son one day. He had a Lego Technic kit with motors and cogs, and took great delight in building a head-mounted cannon that fired plastic Lego studs when you pressed a button (please don't judge us).

He was delighted with the game. Then, noticing that we had a second motor, I started to add another mechanism so that the cannon could be raised and lowered. I got more and more distracted and angry trying to make this ill-conceived contraption work, and after a while I noticed that my son had drifted away and was doing something else. It dawned on me: he just wanted to play, hang out, to be creative and have fun together. No stress, no judgement, no striving. I had turned the game into a chore with a goal to be achieved - it was no longer playful.

Reflect:

Think for a moment about your own attitude to play. How often do you engage in something that you would call *playful*? When was the last time you felt real joy playing?

If your hackles were raised by that question because you are, after all, a serious grown-up, we may need to think about how we define play. Stuart Brown, who has studied play in great depth, suggests that play is doing something without a short term purpose, just for its own sake. "If its purpose is more important than the act of doing it it's probably not play."[1]

One of God's gifts in rest is the chance to stop trying to achieve things, to just enjoy God's world and one another. Play is one of the best ways that we can experience this. Children play instinctively, "just because". They're not banging the spoon on the highchair because they know that they need to develop fine motor skills (which, in the long term, it will teach them), they do it because of the joy of achieving a rhythmic, loud sound. They're not playing shops because they know that to be well-functioning adults it's helpful to rehearse social situations and turn-taking, but because it's a fun game and all sorts of surreal items are for sale in *this* shop. They're not playing rough-and-tumble on the lawn with their siblings because they need to learn consent, develop gross motor skills, how to control physical strength or how to make up after someone gets hurt. They're doing it because it feels like joy in their bodies and because it makes them giggle.

We may not need play like we need food or sleep - it is possible to exist without play. But it would be just that, an existence, not life as God intended for us. When we tell inspiring stories about

---

1   www.ted.com/talks/stuart_brown_play_is_more_than_just_fun

humanity's drive to survive, it's often with examples like the Christmas truce football game in the First World War, orchestras in prisoner of war camps or secret libraries in concentration camps. To survive in any kind of meaningful way, we need to play.

And yet, we struggle to prioritise play, because as goal-driven, efficient adults, we can't see the point. Brown, in his book *Play*, makes a convincing argument that children who are free to play "just because" often become successful, well-balanced adults, whereas those with a deprived play-history often go onto difficult grown-up lives.[2] They're not playing with this goal in mind, but it is nevertheless the result.

True play is not so much childish (if you understand that to mean immature, infantile, inane) but more child-like: demonstrating the good characteristics we can learn from children. And we know that when it comes to being child-like, Jesus says:

> "[...] unless you change and become like little children, you will never enter the kingdom of heaven." (Matt 18:3)

At least part of what it means to become like little children is to learn to play again. Ben Witherington III even makes the case that playing makes us more like God, our spectacularly playful and innovative Creator.[3] Additionally, in joyful play - whether it be in a child's pretend play, a sports game or in playing a piece of music - we are rehearsing for the day when Christ returns - our

2   Stuart Brown, *Play*, (Avery 2010) page 6.

3   Ben Witherington III, *The Rest of Life*, (Eerdmans, 2012) page 42.

Resurrection Day liberation when there will be no more tears, death or fruitless toil (Rev 21:4).

What might play look like for you?

How could your times of rest incorporate something with no immediate goal, something you do simply for the enjoyment of it? It might need to be something not related to your job. For example, we use music a lot in our job, so for music to be playful and restful we need to make sure it's quite different to what we play in church. Sometimes as a family we mess around on instruments we don't really know how to play, attempting pop tunes or Swedish folk songs for no other goal than the fun of it.

Other times we've played with some air-drying clay, making different shapes and models for no definite reason. We have also made use of a book which encourages you to create pictures in the style of famous artists. None of this creativity had any goal other than to enjoy the process.

For some people, playing board games is a great way to relax, unless you're someone who gets very competitive and upset when they lose! For some, exercise is restful, for others it's a competitive slog - try to avoid the type of exercise that makes you feel stressed or wound up.

Respond:

Choose one thing you could do today for the sheer joy of doing that thing. Allow yourself to be playful, even if it is simply for 10 minutes, and then reflect on that experience.

Chapter 26
Rest in Fun

Hands up who thinks that Jesus was fun to be around? I can almost hear the cogs of your brain turning: what is the correct answer to this? On the one hand, *fun* sounds like a good thing, and Jesus was good… but then again, *fun* sounds a little frivolous, and surely Jesus wasn't frivolous? And, importantly, we should take our faith seriously, and you couldn't be serious and have fun at the same time, could you?

We get conflicted about fun as Christians - it has not been part of our discipleship, so we don't know how to reflect on it theologically. There's a sense that if something fun happens in church, a game for the youth group or a quiz night, the fun is used as a tool. It's for evangelistic or fundraising purposes. Fun in itself has little value.

To respond to my original question: I personally believe that Jesus was fun to be around. I have a few reasons for this, but the biggest clue in Scripture is how often kids are mentioned in the gospels.

Palestine in the first century was not a place where children were valued like today, nor did they have many rights. And yet, Jesus picks them out as a particularly precious group.

He became genuinely angry when the disciples tried to stop kids coming up for a blessing (Matt 19), he stood up for children's rights to shout and holler their praise when challenged by the Pharisees (Matt 21), he equated welcoming children with welcoming him (Mark 9) and he stated that children understood the secrets of the Kingdom of God in ways that the "wise" people of the world couldn't (Luke 10).

There seem to be kids hanging around him all the time. And if you've ever met a child, or remember what it is to be a child, you'll know that they are not drawn to serious or grumpy people. They are magnets for fun. They'll find the one grown-up in the group who's happy to play peek-a-boo, throw a ball around or - as we know that Jesus definitely did - tell a funny story. I bet Jesus even did voices.

If this was Jesus, God incarnate, being fun and having fun, could we perhaps consider that fun has God's seal of approval? And as people who believe that we are thoughtfully created by a loving God, it might interest you to know that laughter is scientifically proven to strengthen our immune system, reduce the level of stress hormones in our bodies, relax our muscles, bond with other humans and more.[1] Fun is good for you.

---

1   Elizabeth Scott, PhD, "The Health Benefits of Laughter", engageworship.org/redirect/ BenefitsLaughter

I wonder if even reading this chapter so far has made your shoulders drop just a little bit or perhaps your jaw has unclenched?

Fun Audit

Catherine Price, in her book *The Power of Fun*, defines true fun as having three common denominators: *play* (creative and non-productive), *flow* (where you get into 'the zone', not noticing time passing) and *connection* (with other humans).[2]

One of the most helpful things for me in Price's book is the "Fun Audit" which she encourages her readers to do. It involves plotting the things you do "for fun" in a grid, depending on how enjoyable the activity was and how much energy it generated in you.

I must admit to sometimes having a sense of ill-ease at the mention of fun, because, frankly, what many people think of as fun, I don't find fun at all. The concept of "fun", at least when you're a grown-up, tends to include awkward team-building activities with colleagues or mingle parties where you're required to balance a drink and a plate of *hors d'oeuvres* in your hands, while somehow still being able to shake hands with strangers.

But when I used Price's Fun Audit, those kinds of events ended up as stressful - not fun at all! Also not fun, but at least not stressful, was the four hour dance show I had to sit through in order to see my daughter's absolutely brilliant 5 minute performance. 3 hours and 55 minutes of that event was boring and depressing.

---

2   Catherine Price, *The Power of Fun*, (Bantam, 2021) page 32.

On the more positive scale, there were some nice things that were enjoyable, but not really fun. Things like: having a long, warm bath or getting an hour to myself to read a novel. The two activities that ended up in my sweet spot for True Fun really surprised me - they were not necessarily things that I would have thought of as "fun" things. And yet they clearly ticked Price's three boxes of play, flow and connection.

The first activity was watching a watercolour tutorial with my teenage daughter and sitting shoulder to shoulder with her as we both painted beautiful, and very different, Monstera leaves. My own lone attempts at painting had been enjoyable and nice, but the connection I felt with my daughter pushed our painting session right up to the level of True Fun.

But the activity that felt the most fun in the whole week I'd been plotting my leisure activities was sitting on the floor of our living room chatting with a visiting 9-month old. The call-and-response liturgies of hand-clapping and noise-making, and the delightful way the baby kept finding the same stick of bell-pepper, nibbling it, before losing it again kept me endlessly smiling. I genuinely could have stayed like that for hours.

In those True Fun moments, I wasn't worried about the latest political mess or wars across the world; I wasn't trying to show off or prove anything to anyone; I wasn't judging my daughter's ability to paint or the baby's ability to blow raspberries; my work tasks were momentarily forgotten as I lost myself in the flow of the moment.

Those moments were moments of Sabbath, of ceasing work and striving, of resting in fun.

Reflect:

When did you last experience that kind of true fun which combines play, flow and connection with others?

Are there things you do "for fun", that in reality are stressful, boring or soul-numbing? Can you identify things you ought to try to do less of and any surprising things that might feel like True Fun to you?

How can you add more of this kind of restful fun to your life?

If you struggle to allow yourself to have fun, it might be helpful to spend some time with children, or adults who are particularly playful. Ask God to set you free to play and have fun, to trust that as you enjoy his world you are bringing him glory.

Chapter 27
Rest in the Body

If you picked up this book because you've been feeling a bit stressed or overwhelmed, or because you're sensing that striving and performance has become a too large part of your worship life - how did you experience these feelings? My guess is that they were not just contained to your mind. Even if unexplored or nearly unnoticed, my guess is that you sensed it in your body.

Reflect:

Become aware for a moment now:

- What does stress feel like in your body?
- What does ill-ease feel like?
- What does joy and well-being feel like?

If you don't listen to your body very often, you might have found it hard to answer those questions cohesively. And yet, the experience is still there. You may not have reflected on it, but when someone asks you how you are and you answer "Stressed!", you're really interpreting what your body is telling you. The likelihood is that you're experiencing some combination of sore and tense shoulders, a stomach churning with nausea, an uncomfortable feeling across your chest as your heart races, or other physical symptoms of stress.

In fact, often we feel our emotions in our bodies first, long before we've been able to put words to them. And if we, like so many of us do, continuously ignore what our bodies are trying to tell us, they have the power to halt us, sometimes quite dramatically:

> "If we do not allow for a rhythm of rest in our overly busy life, illness becomes our Sabbath - our pneumonia, our cancer, our heart attack, our accidents create Sabbath for us."[1]

You probably know many people, and unfortunately a fair few in full-time ministry, who have changed their lives into more manageable rhythms, but only after some sort of health scare or burn-out. Wouldn't it be wonderful if we didn't need to get to that point before we rested? If we listened to our bodies before the accidents or illnesses happen?

In my first ever spiritual direction session, the tiny, wrinkled old nun who was listening to me, heard me out and then gave me one piece of "homework" before our next session the following day: "Go and have a nap."

I must admit to having felt a little cheated. I had come prepared for being taught a new prayer practice or given a list of exercises to do. Being asked to go and have a nap felt like the easy answer.

---

1   Wayne Muller, *Sabbath*, (Bantam, 2010) page 20.

"We all need a nap," I thought a little grumpily as I walked away. You probably agree, but let's look at that statement again, in the cold, hard light of day:

We all need a nap.

When you think about it, doesn't it strike you as a little weird? We've sort of come to accept that we're all tired, all of the time. When most of us know all the risks involved in being tired and sleep-deprived.[2] When really, there's a fairly simple solution: sleep and rest more.

Of course, just because something is simple, doesn't mean it's easy. Strangely, despite believing that our bodies are purposefully and intricately created by our loving God, as Christians we are often the worst at treating our physical being well. Stuck in a muddled spirituality influenced by gnosticism and the Enlightenment we often separate and elevate the soul / mind / spirit over the body. And since we have so few helpful role models and have received so little useful Bible teaching on the subject we at best ignore and at worst abuse our bodies.

Separating body from mind, or spirit or soul, is a way of inviting brokenness into our lives. Saundra Dalton-Smith MD says:

> "You are made up of a body, a mind and a spirit. Three unique parts make the whole. Whole is what your body thrives to become. Your body seeks to remember its disjointed relationship with your mind and spirit, and in

---

2   If you need reminding, there's a list of dangers on this page: www.hse.gov.uk/humanfactors/topics/fatigue.htm

doing so remember the sanctity of wholeness."[3]

The sanctity of wholeness. There is holiness in your body being fully integrated with your mind and spirit. There is holiness there, because this wholeness is where God abides.

> "Do you not know that your bodies are temples of the Holy Spirit, who is in you, whom you have received from God? You are not your own; you were bought at a price. Therefore honour God with your bodies." (1 Cor. 6:19-20)

Temples are places for worship - your body is a place where worship takes place! To worship the temple itself is to fundamentally misunderstand what it's there for. Therefore, when you start looking after your body better, you need to have it clear in your mind that this is not in order that *you* might be adored or worshipped. It's so that you become *a better temple*, where worship of the Almighty God can take place.

Honouring God with your body is impossible while you burn the candle at both ends; get too little sleep, water and exercise, and too much junk food, alcohol or drugs. It's time to take the call to whole-person discipleship seriously, it's time for Christians to become the role-models for well-balanced lives.

Often when I feel stressed, physical self-care is the first thing to go. In those times, I find it helpful to imagine that I am outside of myself, looking at myself as another person. I imagine myself as my own child, or my dearest friend, and think about how I would

---

3   Saundra Dalton-Smith MD, *Sacred Rest*, (Faith Words, 2017) page 69.

care for them or advise them in this situation. Because we often treat ourselves in ways that we wouldn't dream of treating our friends, or even our pets.

I'm very aware when I need to tell our children to go to bed, or to just give up on exam revision and go for a walk; and I keep a really careful eye on how well they're eating. And I'm reminded that God, our ever-loving, kind and compassionate parent, looks at me that way too. Desperately wanting me to give myself the best chances of health by giving my body what it needs - sleep, water, nutritious food, exercise.

Reflect:

Take a moment to check in with yourself - how well do you honour God with your body in these different areas? Could you make changes yourself or do you need to ask a friend or a professional for help?

Sleep	Exercise
Food	Hydration

Pray:

One of the ways to re-integrate body, mind and spirit, is to move our bodies when we pray. The second season of our PAUSE / PRAY podcast contains audio reflections that encourage you to pray using your body.[4] Alternatively, spend some time in silence before God in a posture you don't usually pray in: kneeling, lying prostrate, walking, dancing, standing and so on.

---

4   engageworship.org/pausepray

Chapter 28
Rest in Sabbath

Until recently, the concept of "Sabbath" was one of those things of faith that seemed to me to belong to a previous generation of Christians, like dusty hymn books or strict denominational boundaries. In fact, I filed it in a box called "religion" in my mind, a very different box to the "relationship" box where I kept my faith.

All I had learned about Sabbath as a child had to do with optics - we must not *be seen* to be working - and little to do with our inner beings. Because I - Sara - grew up on a farm, where manual labour was the norm, work was the physical, noisy part of the grown-ups' lives. Consequently, there would be no noisy playing on the Sabbath and absolutely, under no circumstances, may we build anything. The most shameful thing, it seemed to me as a child, was if there were echoing sounds of a hammer coming from our den building area. So Sabbath was a day of wearing uncomfortable tights under your uncomfortable Sunday-best dress, spending a lot of time at the village chapel and just generally being shushed a lot.

As a teen and young adult, the idea of Sabbath didn't even cross my mind, especially because church became my work, whether on a paid or voluntary basis. Being sold out for Jesus surely means working every hour for him? If it's ministry, God would provide the strength, right?

If I was God, I'd do a massive eye roll right about now... God *does* provide strength, but more than that, he provides us with wisdom as to how to live so that our strength might last. I used to think of God kind-of like a vending machine for energy drinks, whereas most often he's more like a nutritionist, offering us a menu plan of three healthy meals per day. "Put your life together like this," he says, "and you will last for the long haul."

And so, I'm slowly learning that Sabbath isn't about law; it's not a burden or a dreary performance of righteousness. It's a gift, it's God's wisdom, it's freedom from toil, it's an act of faith and a joy-filled eschatological rehearsal. Let's just refresh our memories of Jesus' beautiful words on the topic:

> "The Sabbath was made to serve us; we weren't made to serve the Sabbath." (Mark 2:27, MSG)

What a wonderful, and clear sentiment! God knows what we need and so he gifted us a day a week to sabbath - to cease work. It's for *our* benefit, not in order to tick boxes or look good. And once we give up on the optics of the Sabbath and understand the heart behind it, we can start to put together a plan of how to observe it. Here are some questions to help you:

What 24 hour period is best for you?

If you work for a church, Sunday is clearly a work day for you and no amount of napping between church services is going to change that. You need to find another day. Monday might feel good after a busy weekend, but if you have family members in education or conventional work hours, Saturday may be your best choice.

The Jewish Sabbath goes from sundown on Friday to sundown Saturday. We have found that going from evening to evening works better for us too, rather than morning until bedtime. So we have quite a busy Saturday, with the children going to groups and doing homework, and the grown-ups trying to finish up life-admin or household chores. But we rarely have plans on a Saturday night, so we can cook a lovely meal to share together to start our Sabbath off. By the time we get to Sunday night, the next week of work starts making itself known, with school uniforms needing ironing and bags needing packing, and so our Sabbath ends then.

What is work to you?

It's reasonably obvious to decide not to do our paid job on a Sabbath. Obvious, but perhaps not always easy. For us it means switching off our work email and closing tabs of workspaces. It means not arranging work meetings, or catching up on work reading or going into the office. Most things can wait for 24 hours.

Of course, there's unpaid work too and this is where you need to make careful decisions about what's helpful and unhelpful to do on a Sabbath. I cook for the family most nights and so rushing home from church to spend hours perfecting a classic British roast dinner is not a restful thing for me. Nor is the oily mountain of washing up left-behind a gift of rest for Sam, our resident washer-upper. So I've made an executive decision for Sunday to be Curry Day in our house, and so we circle through a four-weekly schedule of various Indian and Thai meals, made in advance and frozen.

We may also need to limit other things which feel like work, or can cause us stress. Our 15-year old daughter has a love-hate relationship with her phone. The pressure she feels to chip into group chats or read about the latest drama among her friends has caused her to make a phone-off-for-Sabbath decision.[1]

What to do instead?

Think carefully about what you want your Sabbath to contain (many of the other chapters in this part should be a help). It should be a celebration, not a day of ascetic solitude - so seek connection with others. Turn to God in praise together with others - in church or with those you do life with, be it friends or family.

If you have children, their age and life stage will determine what the best way of being together is. But the most important thing is attention - teach your kids that they are worthy of your full attention, and they will find it much easier to believe in an attentive heavenly Father. When our children were smaller, we used to do "Lego lock-ins", where we tipped out all the Lego in

---

1   See Chapters 13 and 14 for more on digital rest.

the middle of the living room floor and *everyone* had to stay in the room to build - no screens or other distractions. Now that the kids are adolescents, being together looks more like playing board games, going for walks or the occasional creative activity.

Because we're such beginners at Sabbath - the temptation to write to-do lists, get stressed about something or check email is very real - we've put some rituals in place to put boundaries around the 24 hour period. I need a visual reminder that we're in Sabbath mode, so we have a special candle holder made up of a glass jar filled with shells and pebbles from a lovely beach trip, which we move to the middle of the table on Saturday nights. We also exchange our normal mealtime prayer for a Sabbath prayer - I've included it on the next page because it really sums up how to rest on a Sabbath.[2]

2   Used by permission, this prayer was written by Liam Thatcher and can be found here: https://christchurchlondon.org/2021/05/a-prayer-for-sabbath/

God of rest,
today I make the active choice
to enter into your rest,
and to join with you
in delighting in this good world you have made,
and dreaming of the perfect world
you will remake.

I choose to tune out,
of demands and deadlines,
of performance pressures,
of flickering screens,
of that which robs my soul of joy,
and the ways in which the world
seeks to define and shape my identity.

I choose to tune in,
to your affirmation and love,
to the celebration of freedom,
to worship and your word,
to the enjoyment of that
which fills my soul with joy,
and reminds me of my identity in Christ,
as a deeply loved child of God.
Amen.

Liam Thatcher

Chapter 29
Rest in "Quiet Times"

I - Sara - went to an international missions conference when I was 14. It was life-changing for me: meeting young Christians from across the world, learning to sing worship songs in English *and* finding out about a mysterious thing they called "quiet times".

There was a booklet with a page for each day, and an allocated half an hour each morning when we were supposed to engage with this quietly. I was a "good girl" who loved to ace a worksheet, so I got right to it - there was the passage to look up and read, the comments to reflect on, questions with space to write your answers and another space to write your prayer. Tick! Personal relationship with Jesus - done!

This set the tone for my devotional life for years, and if you love tick-lists and being productive like I do, you might also have got used to this formulaic way of approaching quiet times. Or you might have got stuck in a rut of working through a Bible-reading scheme, praying down your intercession list, saying a particular set liturgy or ticking off other things we've been taught to do. All of these can be helpful, especially at first. But eventually the "quiet" can become full of the "noise" of our own activity. Time with God can become another task to achieve rather than a space to grow closer to Jesus. The more of a chore this becomes, the less it will restore our souls.

If we start thinking of our quiet times as a place to nurture relationship with God, rather than to achieve a task, it might help us change our approach. Think, for example, of how you build relationships with friends.

The first requirement is *time*. If you're meeting up with someone, there is nothing worse than them constantly checking their watch and hurrying off at the earliest possible time. Relationships need enough time to move from the shallow chats of everyday life to the deeper sharing of our innermost fears and desires.

Nurturing our relationship with God is no different. Of course we can fire up little prayers of "Thanks!" "Help!" "Praise you!" "God, what?!" throughout the day, just like we might send off short text messages to our friends. But more focussed and extended time is required to truly enter into God's rest.

I am a morning person and it feels important to start my day in extended time with God, but I'm aware that this is not how everyone is wired. Perhaps you could cut out some Netflix time and take 45 minutes at the end of the day with God? Or perhaps your everyday life makes extended times alone with God impossible, especially if you're a carer and there are people relying on you to be available 24 / 7. Could you arrange for some respite for an hour at the weekend, where you just rest with God? If you co-parent, could you gift one another an hour of solitude during Sabbath?

The second thing that seems foundational for true relationship building is an *open agenda*. In conversation with our friends or spouses, we talk and we listen, we give advice and take advice, we are sensitive to how the other person is feeling and the atmosphere in the room. Imagine how our times with God would change if we approached them in the same way?

Coming to God with an open agenda will mean that it will look different every time: sometimes we pour out our hearts, using many words, journalling until our hands cramp; but sometimes we simply sit in silence before the loving gaze of our Father. Sometimes we intercede for others in the most detailed ways and sometimes we just whisper the names of those we love, or light candles in symbolic acts. Sometimes we sit, sometimes we kneel or lie prostrate and sometimes we walk together with God.

Revisiting Bible reading

One other area where our times with God can become formulaic is in how we read the Bible. Ruth Haley Barton makes a comparison between utilising a textbook and reading a love letter.[1] If you take the textbook approach, you're just looking for information. We can skim across large portions of the Bible trying to find the data we need for a sermon we're writing, guidance for a decision, or

---

1   Ruth Haley Barton, *Sacred Rhythms*, (InterVarsity Press, 2006) page 48.

answers to an ethical dilemma. We're interpreting critically and analytically. This is not wrong, but only approaching the Bible in this way falls short of the transforming rest God has for us.

In contrast, with a love letter you pore over the text, taking your time reading and re-reading to draw out every nuance in order that your relationship might grow. You allow yourself to feel the emotions raised by the words, and let them sink into your inner being to change you. Perhaps this offers us a better picture of how we can approach the Bible in our times alone with God.

Lectio divina is an ancient way of reading scripture that encourages this kind of slow reading. You take a short passage and approach God in stillness, asking for him to speak to you.

You *read* that text a number of times, not necessarily to understand or interpret but just spend time with God in his word. You open your heart to God highlighting a particular word or phrase.

Next, turn your attention to that word or phrase. *Reflect* or chew on it, asking God to take you deeper into it. Feel the emotions it inspires. Meditate on how it touches your life in this moment, and be open to the heart of God for you in it.

The third step is to *respond,* talking to God in prayer in response to the word or phrase. That might lead you to thank God, ask for something, say sorry, ask God a question or some other response.

The final step is to *rest.* Having spent this time in God's word, let your words fall away and simply sit in God's presence for a while.

Pray:

Engage in some *lectio divina* now, using the four steps of *read, reflect, respond* and *rest* outlined above. You can use any short passage of the Bible, or start with this:

> "Truly my soul finds rest in God;
> my salvation comes from him.
> Truly he is my rock and my salvation; he is my fortress,
> I will never be shaken." (Ps 62:1-2)

Chapter 30
Rest in Retreat

Imagine for a moment a busy meeting room where the discussion starts getting heated and emotions are heightened. Picture yourself in the middle of this scene, as the noise levels increase, anger flares, sharp words are spoken. "I think I need to step outside for a moment," you might say, and you go outside to breathe some cooler air and let the silence calm you down. You regroup, and eventually are able to think of some new ideas of how to approach the difficult problem being bashed around indoors. You step back into the room.

Going on retreat is a bit like that, except it's not a room full of angry people you're stepping out of, but a life full of demands and distractions. And the cool air you breathe as you regroup is not the oxygen of our earthly atmosphere, but the presence of God, the Holy Spirit, the Breath of Life.

To retreat is to step aside from ordinary time for a little while, stepping out of the hamster wheel of life. Most of us don't do this, however, but keep pushing through instead, always "on", keeping that hamster wheel moving until we fall off in exhaustion or illness. Staying in that room of angry emotions, shouting a little louder to be heard over all the demands. Because none of us have time for a retreat.

> "When should I make a retreat? When there is no time to do it, that's when you most need to unclutter the calendar and go apart to pray. When the gridlock of your schedule forbids it. […] That is when your heart beats against the prison walls of your enslavement and says, 'Yes, Lord, I want to spend time with you.'"[1]

What is your schedule like right now? Does your life feel gridlocked? Is it time to consider stepping outside?

Planning your retreat

Find a retreat to suit you. There are organised retreats around themes (like Advent), media (like art) or spirituality (like Ignatian). There are also retreat houses dotted around the country which have a resident community which you're welcome to join with for a couple of days, without a set programme apart from fixed hour prayer. Some retreat houses offer spiritual direction, which I highly recommend.

I've sometimes been tempted to just go to a cheap hotel for a couple of nights, organising my own retreat, because it'd be cheaper and more convenient. But in my saner moments, this

---

1   Emilie Griffin, *Wilderness Time: A Guide for Spiritual Retreat*, page 17, quoted in Ruth Haley Barton, *Invitation to Retreat*, (InterVarsity Press, 2018) pages 23-24.

strikes me as a bad idea. Being in a space set apart for prayer and communion with God changes the way you approach time. And although I would always prefer a very sparse programme, having no routines or communal times of prayer at all would quickly derail me. I don't make great decisions when I'm tired. And just the thought of the noise level of a breakfast room in a Premier Inn is enough to put me off.

So find a place and a time that is set apart for God. A place where you can eat meals in silent contemplation and there are no demands or distractions. A time when, for once, you can sit with God for extended periods and see what happens; where you can be before his face without an agenda.

What to do on retreat?

Sometimes it might be easier to think about what *not* to do on retreat. Don't bring work and, if you can help it, a laptop. Set your email out-of-office response, or ask a colleague to pick up the slack. Don't go on retreat with the intention of producing or achieving something. Throw away the to-do list.

As Jesus-followers we want to be all about other people; caring, loving and ministering to others. However, during retreat time, allow the time to be solely about you and God. Don't try to network, don't set up meetings and limit who can get in touch with you and how. Smartphones are sometimes as smart as they claim to be, and you can often specify who can get through to you while your phone is set to "Do not disturb".

Engage with your physical being during the retreat time. Nap when you're tired and go to bed early. Move your body gently and lovingly - perhaps take a walk or do some stretching, but hold off on your marathon training or fitness challenge until you're back home.

Don't fill your time or create a full schedule for yourself. At least start the retreat with extended periods of silence, and discover what floats to the surface. This is the opportunity to allow emotions to be felt, rather than shoved down as usual. Sit for a while and feel your emotions and any discomfort, and bring those things before God right at the beginning. "This is me right now," you may want to say to God, "Do with me what you wish in this time."

Read Scripture slowly and meditatively - scrap any crazy "Old Testament in a week" challenge you might be considering. Listen for words that sing to your soul. Pray using less words or no words at all. Perhaps rest in prayers that were written hundreds of years ago, and shake off the need to sound clever.

Wait for God, no rushing ahead. Imagine that you are there, in the upper room and Jesus takes his outer cloak off, all set to wash your feet. Allow him to do that for you.

Respond:

As this part of the book comes to a close, take some time to be still with Jesus as you listen to O *Still My Soul* by Matt Weeks and Calvin Hollingworth, printed on the next page.[2]

---

2   © Matt Weeks Music (admin by ChurchSongs.co.uk) CCLI # 7191560. Listen here - engageworship.org/redirect/OStillMySoul More here - mattweeksmusic.com/murmurs

Jesus still my soul within,
let every noise grow dim,
all but your whisper Lord.
Holy silence fill this space,
the murmurs of your grace,
the stillness of your peace.

Jesus still my restless mind,
it's you I long to find
and to my Anchor hold.
Holy Spirit fill this space,
the warmth of your embrace
the stillness of your peace

O still my soul within,
let every voice of earth grow dim
till I hear only you.
O still my restless mind,
yours is the peace I long to find,
let me hear only you.

Matt Weeks, Calvin Hollingworth

Part Four:
rest in gathered worship

Chapter 31
Negotiating the Giant Helicopter

"Some people see the church as a giant helicopter. They're scared to get too close in case they get sucked into the rotas."

Milton Jones[1]

Have you ever felt like this? That the sheer pace of being involved in church life, being part of the worship team or some other aspect of ministry life is like an endlessly busy vortex, sucking you into more and more activity?

Well, in March 2020, the giant helicopter engines suddenly switched off. Lockdown closed our buildings and cancelled our physical gatherings. A small number of people worked themselves to the bone putting worship services online, while

---

1   "Milton Jones: Stand Up For Jesus" https://www.reform-magazine.co.uk/2013/07/standup-for-jesus/

many others enjoyed the sudden, enforced rest of Sofa Church in the comfort of their pyjamas. In many ways it was less than ideal, but at least for some people it *made* them slow down.

Since society has begun to return to a sense of "normal", we've talked to many pastors and worship team leaders who report the same issue: they can't get people to commit to the rotas any more. Worship leaders and musicians (and other volunteers in youth, family, outreach…) have begun to enjoy their more peaceful Sunday mornings. Family time has blossomed. When you're not over-committed at church, things feel less stressful and pressured.

We entirely sympathise with those who are struggling to fill their ministry rotas. We feel their frustrations of members not committing the ways they used to. And yet, for all the horrors of lockdown and the challenges of post-pandemic life, might it be that we're also being offered a gift? The gift of a pause, a reset, what worship leader Noel Robinson calls the church's "Control+Alt+Delete" moment.[2] Is this a time when we can look at what we've been doing as a church and say: if Jesus invites us to rest, why are we so good at *exhausting* people?

Perhaps part of our problem is the demands we place on the worship life in our churches - how our wants, our preferences, can so easily become our "needs". We so easily slip into thinking: to be able to worship, we *need* these particular songs. We *need* contemporary / traditional music (take your pick!). We *need*

---

2 *Disrupting Worship* podcast episode 2.5, engageworship.org/disrupting-worship

technology, a great sound system, a sharp screen. We *need* a professional worship leader / ordained priest / trained organist.

None of those things are bad in themselves, of course. But we don't truly *need* them to worship. Thankfully, by the grace of God, Christ's death on the cross means access to the Father, by the Holy Spirit. It's *Jesus* who leads us to worship the Father, by the Holy Spirit (Eph 2:18). Christ's death and his continuing intercession at the right hand of the Father are all we need to make worship possible.[3]

In John 6, Jesus' disciples thought that they desperately *needed* a catering company or a fleet of burger vans. They were faced with an impossible situation: thousands of hungry people and a rabbi who told them, his apprentices, to feed the crowd. Eleven of those apprentices focused on the need and what they didn't have. The twelfth, Andrew, looked at what they *did* have. It wasn't much, laughable really, and he may well have felt a little anxious to bring it to Jesus. His friends would probably sneer - his brother Peter undoubtedly so - but somehow Andrew had learned enough about Jesus to dare bring a boy's packed lunch in response to Jesus' request. And of course, we know the end of the story. The little, the not-enough, is offered to Jesus and it becomes enough.

It took a certain vulnerability for Andrew to bring the boy's packed lunch to Jesus. It's a vulnerable thing to look at *what we*

---

3 We expand on this in our book *How Would Jesus Lead Worship* (Music and Worship Foundation, 2020) Chapter 2. Or read James Torrance, *Worship, Community and the Triune God of Grace* (InterVarsity Press 1997). Or the epistle to the Hebrews.

have, rather than *what we want* or think we need. So, we want a rock band, but have a flautist and a beginner keyboard player. We want an organist, but have a guitarist. We want a loud and cheerful congregation, but have a bunch of contemplatives. We want a full-time ordained priest, but have a lay volunteer leader. We want a youth group, but have a church made up mostly of seniors. What does it look like for you to start with what you have, to value it and allow God to work through it?

In this final part of the book we're going to think about how we can approach times of gathered worship in ways that welcome God's rest. Whether you are a pastor, worship leader, or simply a member of the congregation, we'll explore how can we can all play our part in services that allow space for restoration, stillness and peace.[4]

Reflect:

Before we think about our churches, we need to start with our own hearts' posture towards gathered worship. Could we approach God about our church's worship like Andrew did? Say to Jesus: "I thought we needed more, I definitely wanted more, but this is what we have." Offer up a gift of worship out of the little you have, and then leave it in his hands to do the rest.

---

4   For further practical ideas for restful gathered worship: songs, prayers, reflections and a six week sketch for a The Rest Is Worship series, get hold of *The Rest Is Worship: Leaders' Resource eBook*. engageworship.org/RestLeaders

Chapter 32
Rest as Worship

Christians can think of gathered worship as *work*. That might be because they have a job which involves leading worship, or they take seriously their volunteer position on the church worship team. Perhaps we've thought about the importance of worship forming and shaping the congregation, and therefore the vital work involved in choosing and leading the right mix of words and resources. It could be that we've reflected on worship as a sacrifice, the conscious effort involved in giving glory and praise to God. Or maybe we have focused on the importance of our worship changing the world as we declare and intercede.

All of those things are good, important and true. But could it be that somewhere along the line worship has become *all* about work? Have we made worship something that we achieve, rather than a gift that we receive?

Theologian Miroslav Volf describes worship as "adoration and action", two very active terms.[1] "Adoration" is primarily the devotion and praise we give to God in church gatherings. "Action" is how we glorify God through serving him in our lives and work. Having established the importance of these, Volf then goes on to say there is a third aspect to worship, which he calls "reception":

> "We can give God only what we have first received from God. Reception is, therefore, a third dimension of Christian life that is even more fundamental than action and adoration... Christians are *receivers*."[2]

Giving to God in worship relies on us being willing to also *receive* from God. In order to act, to carry out the work of worship, we also need to rest, to pause, and to allow God to do the work. Ben Quash writes:

> "It is true that the root meaning of the Greek word 'liturgy' is work, but [...] the familiar idea of work has been turned on its head when it turns into worship. Worship is the *Lord's* work."[3]

Worship involves work, but it is also a gift from God that we receive in rest.

This way of thinking can inspire us to reconsider some of our models when we approach gathered worship. We might want to

---

1   We adapted these categories into "gathered worship" and "scattered worship" in our book *Whole Life Worship*, (IVP, 2017) page 20.

2   Miroslav Volf "Worship as Adoration and Action" in Carson (ed), *Worship: Adoration and Action*, (Paternoster Press, 1993) page 211.

3   Ben Quash, *Abiding*, (Bloomsbury Continuum, 2012) page 81.

look for some different resources, and be inspired by movements other than just the ones we see on YouTube or at conferences.

Most traditions have aspects of worship which lean towards simple receiving. For example, Charismatics have the model of "soaking worship", where worshippers rest in God's presence as quiet background music is played and occasional bits of scripture are read. In a lot of ways this isn't so different from the simple, repeated chants you will find at the Taizé community in France. Contemplative Christianity has given us the idea of "centring prayer", resting in God's presence while using short phrases repeatedly in time with our breath.

The Society of Friends (or "Quakers") have no music or formal prayer in their worship, but simply sit in silence and wait on a word from God. One of their poets, John Greenleaf Whittier, wrote a long poem in which he responded to what he saw as the emotionalised, frenzied musical worship of his day. He concludes by asking the "Dear Lord and Father of mankind" to "forgive our foolish ways". He asks God to help us meet with him in stillness, quietness and rest. The end of the poem was eventually set to music and became a very popular hymn.

Reflect: Take a moment to pause and receive from God as you reflect on the verses on the next page.[4]

---

4 Jubilate Hymns version of *Dear Lord and Father of Mankind*, John Greenleaf Whittier (1807 - 1892) © Jubilate Hymns Ltd, used by permission.

O sabbath rest by Galilee!
O calm of hills above,
when Jesus shared on bended knee
the silence of eternity
interpreted by love,
interpreted by love!

With that deep hush subduing all
our words and works that drown
the tender whisper of your call,
as noiseless let your blessing fall
as fell your manna down,
as fell your manna down.

Drop your still dews of quietness,
till all our strivings cease;
take from our souls the strain and stress,
and let our ordered lives confess
the beauty of your peace,
the beauty of your peace.

John Greenleaf Whittier

Chapter 33
Simplify

Back in 1997 Soul Survivor church in Watford was one of the most exciting, vibrant churches in the UK: packed with young people, cutting-edge worship leaders and bands, and running major Christian festivals. But pastor Mike Pilavachi sensed something was not quite right.

> "In our hearts we marked the worship out of ten: 'Not that song again', 'I can't hear the bass', 'I like the way she sings'. It was as if the outcome of the session depended on the people who were up on the stage, as if they were responsible for making it a good or bad time of worship."[1]

So Mike took drastic action. He banned the band. He dismantled the PA system. If people wanted to worship, it had to come from their hearts. It had to come from within the congregation. And it had to be empowered - not by music or technology - but by the Spirit.

---

1   Mike Pilavachi with Craig Borlase, *For The Audience Of One*, (Hodder & Stoughton, 1999) page 134.

Worship leader Matt Redman admits that initially he was a bit offended at being stood down. But over time he realised that "some of the things we thought were helping us in our worship were actually hindering us."[2] He admits that initially the services were quite uncomfortable, but gradually the congregation began to re-learn simple worship from their hearts. It was out of this experience Matt wrote the now classic song *Heart of Worship (When the Music Fades)*.

That story has long been an inspiration for us. On a number of occasions in different churches, we have led seasons where we intentionally allowed the music to fade and some of the complications and technology to be stripped away. When we have removed some of those things, we've created space for God to work in our hearts in a new way.

I - Sam - know that I find it really easy to rely on external things to worship: choosing and rehearsing the right songs, organising the screen and PA. If I'd been there with Paul it might have made quite a different version of Acts 16. You probably know the story: Paul and Silas are thrown in jail. They are about to start worshipping, which will lead to an earthquake and the prison doors opening and the jailer coming to Christ. But then I would pipe up: hang on guys, none of us have a guitar, we haven't got a projection screen and we can't get on YouTube...

People sometimes say to us: "We can't worship in our home group, we don't have any musicians", or "We don't have anyone in our

---

2   Matt Redman, *The Unquenchable Worshipper*, (Kingsway, 2001) page 76.

church skilled with the technology we need for worship". When did worship get so complicated? When did it start to require so many trained leaders, or a large and complex technological setup?

Music, technology, liturgy, creativity, trained leaders - these are all good things which can bless congregations and glorify God. But we know, ultimately, that these are not the things that *make worship happen.* It is possible that we can surround worship with technological production, liturgical correctness, or creative spectacle to the point where the heart of worship is obscured or even lost entirely.

Think back to the most meaningful times of worship you have experienced. Some of them might have been grand, extravagant services in cathedrals, conferences or festivals. But I bet you can also think of some very simple times of worship - breaking bread around a kitchen table, singing around a camp-fire, praying quietly with a friend when you were in a difficult situation. Your mind might go to when you met God out on a walk in nature, when you sat in a silent chapel, or when someone simply spoke a word from the Bible that touched your heart.

Embracing the rest which Jesus offers us may well involve re-thinking our expectations of what we do when we gather to worship. There are times for lavish celebrations: conferences and festivals, Easter Sunday, Christmas carol services, church anniversaries, baptisms and so on. Those are great times to pull out all the stops and use every bit of creativity, technology and complexity at our disposal.

But we want to suggest that perhaps, on a regular Sunday morning, churches might do well to consider simplifying their worship, making it *sustainable*. The expectation of festival style services every week can wear our leaders and volunteers down. And we may find that highly complex worship does not always provide the restoration our souls crave. In simple worship, when the music fades and all is stripped away, we may well find the rest in God we need.[3]

Reflect:

Spend some time in silence reflecting on your own attitude to gathered worship. Are there things, like special people, music or rituals, that you rely on in order to feel like you've worshipped? Bring these thoughts to God. Allow him to assure you that you are able to come to him through Christ alone.

---

3   See more practical ideas for this in *The Rest Is Worship: Leaders' Resource eBook*, Chapter 1. engageworship.org/RestLeaders

Chapter 34
Just a Little Bit

Music for contemporary worship is often a wall of sound, all the sonic spaces taken up with loops and pads and layers of instrumentation (of course, previous generations have done the same thing with enormous church organs). We visually saturate people with videos and lights. We carefully programme services so there is minimal "dead time", slickly segueing from one item to the next.

I know that in my own planning of worship I've often taken the approach that I am responsible for filling 100% of the time, the space, the audible and visual bandwidth. But a few years ago I heard a recording of Henri Nouwen speaking which challenged my attitude. He said this:

> "That's what liturgy [gathered worship] is about. A little bit of bread, but not enough to take hunger away. A little wine, but not enough to take all thirst away. A few words, but not enough to take ignorance away. It's a little bit, and

it creates some boundaries where we are poor together. We sing a song - it's useless! We read a little reading, it's not saying everything. We take a little piece of bread, a little sip of wine, and we are silent. I think words, and songs, and everything we do are to create a safe silent place, where we can hold hands around an empty spot and trust there God will reveal himself to us."[1]

Nouwen seems to be suggesting the opposite of the 100% approach. He speaks honestly, admitting that what he brings to the table is, I don't know, 10%? 25%? A bit of bread and wine, but not enough to satisfy. Some words, but they're insufficient. A song - useless! This is not about being ill-prepared or slapdash or uncreative in our planning and leading of worship. It is about a kind of humility which says "I am not the one making this worship *happen.*" What we do as human beings is never the full story of leading people into worship.

We bring our gifts, our time, our creativity, and I think God delights in these offerings. Yet we need to acknowledge that they arc never enough. It's Jesus who leads us to the Father, in the power of the Holy Spirit. It's God who makes our worship *happen.* And, importantly, it may be that our 100% approach is actually *hindering* worship. If musicians, technicians and leaders fill all the musical, visual and temporal space, where is the room for us to gather and recognise our poverty, our need, our desperation for God to graciously make his presence known with us?

---

1   Henri Nouwen, talk via *Henri Nouwen - Now and Then* podcast. https://henrinouwen.org/listen/henri-nouwen-1992/

I believe that simplifying, relying on God more and our own abilities less, might just reduce the stress and pressure of leading worship. It might open up worship leading to include other people with less "obvious" gifts. And it might draw the exhausted back into our Sunday gatherings.

You may or may not feel like a worship leader. But I expect that, even if you're not involved with services, there are times when you would like to facilitate people connecting with God. That might be in your home group, or around your dinner table. It might be with the elderly or a group of children.

The good thing is, if Nouwen is right, you don't need musical skills or theological training. You bring that "little bit" that creates a space where you can be poor together, and that opens up the opportunity for God to come and do the rest.

We talk about restful singing in Chapter 36, but here are a few other practical ideas which involve no music at all for leading people into worship:

Lean on the Bible.[2] Read a psalm, slowly. Maybe start with Psalm 23. You could all read together, or have one person read and the others listen. Give space for reflection between each section, or invite people to respond to the words of the psalm in prayer in those gaps. Or take some words of Jesus and repeat them with different emphases:

---

2   See Chapter 38 for other ways to worship with the Bible.

> "*Peace* I leave with you; my *peace* I give you [...] *Do not* let your hearts be troubled and *do not* be afraid."

> "Peace *I* leave with you; *my* peace *I* give you [...] Do not let *your* hearts be troubled and do not be afraid."

> "Peace I leave with *you*; my peace I give *you* [...] Do not let your hearts be *troubled* and do not be *afraid*." (John 14:27)

Leave silence. Invite your group to be still, allowing them the gift of some time in silence. Here you are not trying to achieve anything more than simply being in God's presence.[3]

Expect to meet with God in bread and wine. The Emmaus pair's eyes were opened when Jesus broke the bread. Do you expect to meet with Jesus in communion as much as when you sing, or hear the Bible read and preached? You could follow Nouwen's advice: "We take a little piece of bread, a little sip of wine, and we are silent [...] hold hands around an empty spot and trust there God will reveal himself to us."

---

3   See Chapter 37 for more on silence.

Chapter 35
A Local Church Story

The local church that we'd made our home, that we'd poured ourselves into and loved dearly, was closed down during the Pandemic. During a period of mourning and confusion, we wrestled with where to go next. St Luke's Leagrave wasn't the nearest church, it didn't have the coolest band or the flashiest building. But what we found was an extraordinary group of very ordinary, imperfect people, embracing the welcome and rest of Jesus. In this chapter we want to paint a picture for you of what we've experienced - not that your church will be the same, but to give you a sense of what rest in corporate worship might feel like.

Firstly, although as musicians and worship leaders we naturally want to use our skills to help the church, this is the first church we've ever been part of where it has felt entirely okay to say "no" to some things. We know that our vicar, Grace, and consequently the rest of the church, value us as people, not as resources. Milton Jones' fear of being "sucked into the rotas" is not an issue.

Grace organises rotas for some things that take a bit of preparation, like preaching or leading the service. But for many other tasks, the St Luke's way is to invite people to step up on the day. Grace had wanted to include more children and young people in the services, but read somewhere that creating rotas for them becomes almost impossible because life gets in the way. So the service leader will often approach someone before the service and ask them if they can help. Regularly, this even happens from the front - "Who can bring up the offering plate / light the candles / lead the call-to-worship this morning?" - and it feels inclusive and welcoming, rather than unplanned or chaotic.

Secondly, St Luke's is part of the Church of England, but it manages to avoid the ditches of either rebelliously throwing off all Anglican liturgy, nor legalistically adhering to tradition for its own sake. After the first time of witnessing Grace lead a service, Sara remarked that she wears her Anglicanism like a comfy jumper, rather than a straight-jacket.

Grace inherited a fairly formal Sunday morning service, with lots of different books and many, many words. Identifying this as a source of stress for her, she soon worked down to one, simpler sheet of paper each week. She told us that she reached a point in the middle of leading a service where she suddenly thought "I'm so sick of my own voice!" Her advice to anyone who finds themselves in that place is to be curious about what you're feeling. The likelihood is that if you're bored with your voice as a leader, the congregation may be too!

The order of service was simplified further after Lockdown,

having realised that people were responding well to less words and a slower pace. Our service now centres around a small number of key, repeated prayers and actions. Their regular use gives a stability to the service, and creates a platform for contributions, playful spontaneity and the occasional creative idea.[1]

Thirdly, this simplified service order allows space for us not to rush, and keeps things short. Luton, the town we live in, is full of people working hard to stay afloat, balancing several jobs with various life crises, immigration struggles or care commitments. So Grace has shortened the services to somewhere between 45 minutes to an hour. People can trust that if they make the commitment to turn up on a Sunday, they will get to take part in a meaningful, restful worship experience, and they won't be held hostage to the preacher, leader or musician's egos.

Similarly, St Luke's is not a church full of meetings. If something important happens like an AGM, commissioning or celebration, it generally happens on a Sunday morning when we're all there, and other things will be cut to make room.

Fourthly, the atmosphere is primarily relational. The congregation is mostly seated around tables, with the coffee and tea station open throughout the service. Children are free to move around, there are baskets of fiddle toys available, and Grace sets a wonderful example in the way she handles her own children who will occasionally need a hug from her, even if it happens to be in the middle of the Lord's Prayer. Grace says:

---

1   Read more about the benefits of repeated prayers, often accompanied by physical movements, in the *Leaders' Resource eBook*, Chapter 4. engageworship.org/RestLeaders

"My approach to ministry is all relational. I need to get to know the congregation and they need to get to know me, and I need to know their story. [...] Understanding the families where both parents work for the NHS, or that someone is going through bullying at work, or that someone is grappling with unemployment: you have to know and value their lives, as you seek to value your own."

Grace has an intimate knowledge of needing rest. Part of her story includes becoming diagnosed and bedridden with Chronic Fatigue Syndrome in the middle of her ordination training. This came after a very busy time in her 20's doing everything and being involved everywhere. Suddenly her body said "stop".

If you meet Grace, ask her about how God miraculously healed her, it's a wonderful story! But when she came out of that time, she had to recalibrate how she functioned, she had to work out how to pace herself and to accept this, not as a weakness to be fought, but as part of how God made her. This experience has shaped her ministry and the church she leads.

Reflect:

Your church will be different to ours, but are there principles from this story you could apply to your own situation?

Chapter 36
Restful Singing

Singing is central to the vast majority of churches' worship. We've already noted that for many church leaders it is has become increasingly demanding to organise technologically driven and musically complex times of singing. But perhaps we've forgotten just how simple church music can be. In fact, every person in the congregation carries around an instrument with them at all times: their voice! It ought to be possible to show up together and just *sing.*

You may read that and experience mixed emotions. Some people are very self-conscious about their singing voice. We might have been told by teachers, parents or other influential people that we "can't sing"; some have experienced the humiliation of being asked to leave a choir or being told to "pipe down".

But the truth is, *your voice matters to God.* There are at least 50 encouragements in the Bible to sing together. Human parents, at least on their good days, love to hear the voices of their children.

And God is our *perfect* parent, who delights when we sing to him. Infants most often sing naturally before they speak, and it is only our "professionalised" Western music culture that separates people into groups of singers and (allegedly) non-singers.

If you worry that your one individual voice could feel thin, unconfident or out of tune, be encouraged that something magical happens when a group of people sing together. As John Bell puts it, group singing brings:

> "the unique blending of high and low voices, sharp and flat, sophisticated and rough-tongued, male and female, old and young [...] So if we can sense it, every time a congregation sings it is offering an absolutely one-time-only gift to its maker."[1]

Does that change how you view making music together? You are an indispensable part of the body of Christ, an essential and unique part of the choir of Christ. It matters that you show up, open your mouth and make a joyful noise.

Singing together has also been shown to have many restful benefits for humans. It releases oxytocin which will "reduce stress, anxiety and increase feelings of trust and well-being".[2] As we choose to join in with the same words and tune, a remarkable act of unity can occur:

> "As we sing together we belong to one another in the

---

1   John L Bell, *The Singing Thing*, (Wild Goose Resource Group, 2000) page 80-81.

2   Maya Rogers, *The Healing Power Of Your Voice*, https://diymusician.cdbaby.com

song. We agree, in effect, not to be soloists, self-absorbed mediators, or competitors, but to compromise with each other, join our voices as if joining hands, listen to each other, keep the same tempo, and thus love each other in the act of singing."[3]

Singing community songs

It is worth noting that is a difference between "performance songs" and "community songs". For example, take *Happy Birthday*. It is not the most inspiring piece of music to listen to, but we can all join in with it, and the person we're singing to feels celebrated. The melody is well-known, its rhythms are steady and predictable, and the tune falls within an accessible range.

There are probably worship songs you love from hearing them on the internet or at conferences. They will likely be backed by large music groups, played by skilled instrumentalists and sung by professional vocalists. There is nothing wrong with these songs. But have you noticed that often when you try to sing some of them in your local church, or at a home group, they can feel difficult to follow, or lack the energy of the recorded version? It is likely that these are not ideal community songs.[4]

What would you sing if you were stuck in prison with Paul and Silas, or at the Last Supper with Jesus? The chorus of a well-known hymn might come to your mind. A simple 1980's worship song with just one verse might bubble up. Or perhaps the refrain

---

3   Brian Wren, *Praying Twice*, (Westminster John Knox Press, 2000) page 84.

4   For more practical tips and song ideas, see our *Leaders' Resource eBook* Chapters 2 and 3. engageworship.org/RestLeaders

of a modern song. Grab hold of these simple, memorable kinds of music and you may find that singing is released in your community.

There also are many songs from non-Western cultures that can be a great resource for simple singing. One of the great things about the internet is that it can offer us a much wider choice of music, but we have to be intentional about seeking out varied songs from other cultures. Songs that have been written with group singing in mind include: the chants of the Taizé community, intentionally written to unite teenagers from across the world;[5] short songs from the Iona Community;[6] the haunting minor tune to *Kyrie Elieson* written by Dinah Reindorf from Ghana;[7] the call-and response *Gloria* from Peru.[8]

Respond:

Choose to sing a song to God - a simple song, whatever is on your heart. You might want to choose the simple song we've written as part of this project, *In The Presence Of The Holy*,[9] or another song. Know that God loves to hear you sing.

---

5 engageworship.org/redirect/taize

6 engageworship.org/redirect/iona

7 engageworship.org/redirect/reindorf

8 engageworship.org/Glory_To_God

9 © Gemma & Timo Scharnowski, Sam Hargreaves, admin by ChurchSongs.co.uk CCLI # 7212380. Listen here - engageworship.org/InThePresence

In the presence of the holy
may my words be few.
In your presence, I give glory,
there is none like you.

Hallelujah, hallelujah,
there is none like you.
Hallelujah, hallelujah,
there is none like you.

Gemma & Timo Scharnowski,
Sam Hargreaves

Chapter 37
Silence in Gatherings

"The Lord said, 'Go out and stand on the mountain in the presence of the Lord, for the Lord is about to pass by.' Then a great and powerful wind tore the mountains apart and shattered the rocks before the Lord, but the Lord was not in the wind. After the wind there was an earthquake, but the Lord was not in the earthquake. After the earthquake came a fire, but the Lord was not in the fire. And after the fire came a gentle whisper. When Elijah heard it, he pulled his cloak over his face and went out and stood at the mouth of the cave." (1 Kgs 19:11-13)

Often it can feel like worship needs the storm of an energetic preacher, the earthquake of a sub-bass rhythm, or the fire of a light show to bring the presence of God into our services. However in this story God speaks in a gentle whisper, or some translations say "a still, small voice" or "the sound of sheer silence".

Elijah has lived a contemplative life, exiled in the wilderness of

Kerith and Zarephath (1 Kgs 17). He has learned to hear the still, small voice of God. When he has his showdown with the prophets of Baal, we see them shout, scream, dance, even slash themselves to try and get Baal's attention. Elijah's response is comical:

> "'Shout louder!' he said. 'Surely he is a god! Perhaps he is deep in thought, or busy, or travelling. Maybe he is sleeping and must be awakened.'" (1 Kgs 18:27).

Elijah knows that we don't need to wake God up. We don't need to play louder music, sing and dance more energetically, pray with more fervour, give more sacrificially, light up the pyrotechnics or punish our bodies to please him. At Carmel, Elijah prays a simple prayer, and God answers. At Horeb, Elijah waits through the noise and wonders to hear God whisper in the silence. When we come to God, he's already there, speaking. We might just need to get quiet enough to listen.

Silence is free. It requires no musicians or technology. We wrote about the blessings of silence for our daily lives in Chapter 22, but church leaders can be very hesitant to allow times of silence in services. We can be concerned that people will find it awkward, or that there will be noises or interruptions.

Our vicar, Grace, told us that in her 20's rest and silence were alien to her. Then she spent a year as part of the Taizé ecumenical community in France. Here, during their worship, a short Bible reading in multiple languages is followed by an extended time of silence. She said that in the midst of the busyness and pressures of community life:

"You would long for those times of worship, three times a day, when you'd know there would be 10 minutes of silence. That really opened me up to see that yes, life is demanding, but when you take those times aside to pray, to be still, you start encountering God's rest."

Thousands of other teenage pilgrims who gather from all over the world have also reported that this is a particularly important part of Taizé's gathered worship. One author comments:

"When young people first come to Taizé, the time of silence is too long, but by the time they leave, it's too short."[1]

Could this be an encouragement for you and your congregation? Perhaps to begin with your church may feel anxious or fidgety during silence, but over time you may look forward to it as a vital part of your week with God. Experiment with reading a short passage before a time of silence. Afterwards, you could invite people to share any things they were reflecting on, or that they sensed God highlighting in the text.[2]

Pray:

Experiment with this for yourself. Read the following passage and then just sit in silence with God, allowing this to be as much praise and prayer as if you were singing or speaking.

"Silence is praise to you, Zion-dwelling God, and also obedience. You hear the prayer in it all." (Ps 65:1, MSG)

---

1   Jason Brian Santos, *A Community Called Taizé*, (InterVarsity Press, 2008) page 41.

2   For more see *Leaders' Resource eBook*, Chapter 6. engageworship.org/RestLeaders

Chapter 38
Contemplative Worship

It had been a busy week. Deadlines at work. Travelling for meetings. Running kids to clubs. Seemingly endless household chores and life admin. We arrived at church a bit out of sorts, our minds distracted with the regrets and struggles of the past week and pre-occupied with the week ahead.

We were greeted and an opening video was shown. Then, instead of rushing on, the service leader paused and drew our attention to one line from the video: that Jesus wanted to meet us "in the everyday mess of our homes". There was stillness as the congregation took the time to reflect on whatever mess they had come from, the joys and challenges of the week gone by. I felt my shoulders relax, my breathing slow, the tears begin to come. Candles were lit, a prayer was said. Worship provided a space to be present.

To contemplate is simply to reflect, to be present and pay attention to the people, the things and the moment in front of us. The

Christian contemplative tradition has many gifts to help us regain this sense of attention. Mark Yaconelli writes,

> "Contemplation is about presence. It's about attentiveness - opening our heart's eye to God, ourselves and others."[1]

Many contemplative practices flow down from the Desert Mothers and Fathers, who moved out of the cities around the 3rd Century to pursue a simpler lifestyle in the Egyptian desert. They were inspired by the life of Jesus and in particular his time in the wilderness. Soon, many came to join them, and their way of life and acts of worship became the basis of monastic communities.

This tradition has rich resources to offer us today, not only in our personal times with God but also as we gather together. In fact, experiencing reflective worship on a Sunday is a great way of giving us tools we can use through the week.

Our PAUSE / PRAY podcasts are simple ways to begin to explore this kind of worship for yourself. In those episodes we combine reflective music with Bible meditations, in ways that you can use personally, or play to a group.[2] Here are some further ideas you can try.[3]

Examen

The prayer of *examen* comes from St Ignatius. One way to approach it is like this: begin by stilling yourself and becoming

---

1   Mark Yaconelli, *Contemplative Youth Ministry*, (SPCK, 2006) page 6.

2   engageworship.org/pausepray

3   We unpack ideas for contemplative worship with a congregation further in the *Leaders' Resource eBook*, Chapter 6. engageworship.org/RestLeaders

aware of God's presence. Think back on the blessings of the past day, and express gratitude to God for those things. Then reflect on what has been a challenge: what emotions did these more difficult things bring up? How did you respond to those things? Talk to God about this. Finally, think ahead to what is coming up next for you, and hand these things and yourself over to God. This can be adapted for a group or a whole congregation: perhaps at the beginning of a worship time reflecting back on the week, or after a talk to think through its application.

Contemplating the Bible

Rather than rushing through a Bible reading with the expectation that the preacher will explain it to us, contemplative spirituality invites us to slow down and chew on scripture, to marinate ourselves in it and allow God to speak in the moments as we read or listen.

In Chapter 29 we talked about *lectio divina* as a way to do this as an individual. For groups and congregations, a development of this is called "Dwelling in the Word".[4] We led this for a whole month in one church we were part of, in place of a sermon slot.

It works like this: the passage is read aloud (possibly two or three times) and also made available in printed or projected form. A few minutes of silence are held, creating space for God to speak to people through the text. Each person is then invited to share with a neighbour what they heard in the text. Finally, everyone is given opportunity to feedback to the whole group. The twist is that

---

4   churchmissionsociety.org/blog/dwelling-in-the-word/

people don't share what *they* said, they have to share what their neighbour said (this encourages good listening!). In our church we wrote all these things on a flipchart, and reflected together on what God had spoken to us as a community.

Visio divina. A further development of those ways of reflecting on the Bible is to use visual art, in what has been called *visio divina*. This could work really well in a small group, or could be for a whole congregation. Follow the pattern outlined above, but as well as reading a passage put up one or more pictures related to the text. You could use art made by someone in your community, or some of the visual images offered on our website.[5] Another great resource for this is the Visual Commentary on Scripture.[6] Here, for each passage, curators have been tasked with choosing three contrasting images from traditional and contemporary art, and from a wide range of cultures. This provides rich and surprising new ways to "see" God's word.

Pray:

Engage in some *visio divina* for yourself. Make use of the Visual Commentary on Scripture or a physical visual artwork relating to a Bible passage. Sit with the artwork long enough to allow God to speak to you in the stillness.

5   engageworship.org/images

6   thevcs.org

Chapter 39
Play and Fun in Gathered Worship

Coming together to worship with your church family can feel different on different days. Sometimes it can feel soothing and peaceful and other times sombre and profound. Sometimes - and especially if we're involved in leading or playing - it can feel quite stressful and a lot like work. There are times when it just feels dead and meaningless. Occasionally, it can feel life-giving and playful - those are some of my favourite times.

We talked in Chapter 25 about how play is a tool to help us rest in God, because it's not about achieving, but about finding flow in the present moment. Corporate worship ought to have those characteristics. Theologian Romano Guardini wrote:

> "[Worship] has one thing in common with the play of a child and the life of art - it has no purpose, but is full of

profound meaning. It is not work, but play."[1]

Marva Dawn called worship a "royal waste of time" in her book of the same name. Worship is not there to achieve an immediate, utilitarian goal, it's there in the first place simply for us to take joy in God and God to take joy in us. For us to respond to his invitation to be with him. In worship, we delight to be with God and with God's people, we sing and move and tell stories as his children at play in his presence.

Just as a child plays because connections are sparked in their mind and soul and play just bubbles up, so we worship because it simply flows from our hearts. God reveals himself, sparking connections and creativity in our minds, and our souls respond in praise.

The times when worship perhaps has felt dead are likely to have been times when the purpose of the act has become more important than the act itself: great focus has been on *sounding good*, getting the harmonies perfect or the words annunciated well. Or the *theological formation* has become the focus to such an extent that the worship becomes filled to the brim with difficult words and concepts. Or a nervous leader tries so hard to fulfil the demands of their particular style or denomination, that *doing it "right"* becomes the end goal.

Reflect:
Can you identify times when the purpose of the act of worship

---

1   Romano Guardini, *The Spirit of the Liturgy*, quoted by Dr James R Heart in "Worship As Play", Worship Leader https://worshipleader.com

has been more important than the act itself? When in corporate worship have you experienced playful freedom?

Unfinished

When worship becomes a corporate act with high congregational participation, rather than a performance from the front, it suddenly sparks into life. You can watch someone singing a worship song on YouTube any day, but to join an act of worship in person where we *all* get involved is a special, unique and life-generating thing.

The Christian church started off entirely interactive - Paul tells the Corinthians:

> "When you come together, everyone has a hymn, or a word of instruction, a revelation, a tongue or an interpretation. All of these must be done for the strengthening of the church." (1 Cor 14:26)

Despite this initial interactivity, church all too quickly became a spectator sport. This can be true in cathedrals, in arena-style worship with lights and smoke machines, as well as very ordinary, middle-of-the road kinds of churches. A more playful approach to worship involves loosening the reins a little and giving other people space to shape the experience.

We like this little quote by music producer Brian Eno, where he states why he dislikes the word "interactive": "*unfinished* is a better word: It implies that you, the user, are also the maker of the experience."[2]

---

2   Interview in *Wired* magazine. www.wired.com/2008/05/st-15th-eno/

When we come to worship, what a wonderful, playful and restful thing it would be if more of it was unfinished; if I arrived at church believing that my presence there made a difference; that there was space for my praise, questions, struggles, passions and creativity. It takes some work on behalf of the leader to open up safe space for spontaneous contributions from the congregation, but the rewards are great.[3]

True Fun in worship

We'll close with a thought from the book *The Power of Fun* we referred to back in Chapter 26. Here Catherine Price defines True Fun as being a moment when *playfulness*, *connection* and *flow* converge.[4] I read that and immediately thought "that describes a really good time of worship!" and you might agree. She does, however, also highlight the two main enemies of true fun: *distraction* and *judgement*. And again, I thought, "yes, those kill worship dead".

If everyone is checking their phones, being bored and thinking about their dinner or - dare we say - the performance from the front is so spectacular that the performer becomes the focus, we are distracted from God and from the act of worshipping together.

Similarly, if we don't dare to pray out loud because we think we might be judged on our language or theology, or if only professional singers or musicians get to take part, the judgement

---

3   Find practical ideas for fun, playful and unfinished worship in our *Leaders' Resource eBook*, Chapter 7. engageworship.org/RestLeaders

4   Catherine Price, *The Power of Fun*, (Bantam, 2021) page 32.

in the room renders playful worship impossible.

But when there is a sense of flow, when everyone finds a connection and when playfulness is allowed to arise in worship, spectacular things can happen.

Have a go!

How can you be a catalyst for playful worship today? Could you send a message to your WhatsApp prayer group with something like "Let's worship God through the alphabet - I'll start: God is Awesome..."? Could you paint a Bible verse and pop it in the post for someone? Could you suggest to your church that you open the floor for praise from the congregation on Sunday?

Chapter 40
Living Freely and Lightly

To rest in God is to worship, and gathered worship can be a place of God's restoration. This is the invitation that we have sensed God offering to us, and that we have sought to pass on to you.

As we have begun to live out of God's gift of rest, the following hymn lyrics emerged (set to the tune Slane, known for *Be Thou My Vision*). It sums up much of our journey and the journey of this book, so we invite you to spend some time with these words now. Read them through and, if you like, listen to our recording of this hymn, or just sing it yourself.[1]

As you do so, think about what God has been saying to you about rest. What has been a challenge to you from this book? What has been an encouragement? What difference might this make to your life, your work, your ministry? What might be your practical next steps?

---

1   *Lord May Our Resting* © Sam Hargreaves, admin by ChurchSongs.co.uk
CCLI # 7212311. Listen here engageworship.org/LordMayOurResting

Lord may our resting be worship to you,
to lay down our labour and give you your due,
to walk by still waters where souls are restored,
to turn from our striving and trust you are Lord.

Give us the strength to switch off and unplug,
releasing distractions that grip like a drug,
embracing the fullness of life beyond screens;
to be in the moment, to breathe and to dream.

We may be anxious of what we will find,
the fears that the silence may bring to our minds,
but there in the stillness we hear your true voice:
we're loved and accepted, your treasure, your joy.

May our inaction bring freedom and praise,
resisting the powers that keep us enslaved;
we're precious, not measured by work we have done,
not human resources but daughters and sons.

May this, your Sabbath, be worship divine,
a temple of peace, a cathedral of time;
for whether a minute, an hour or a day
you hallow the moments we rest in your name.

Sam Hargreaves

As you come to the end of this book, it is our hope and prayer that you will have heard the whisper of Jesus: "Come all you weary and burdened and I will give you rest." Whatever your burdens, whatever is making you weary, you can lay all of that down before Jesus.

Jesus offers us "unforced rhythms of grace" - natural, life-giving rhythms of work and rest, community and solitude, engagement and Sabbath. How can you begin to live more fully in those rhythms?

He loves to use you, he loves to see you work and sacrifice for him. But you're not a "human resource" in his project: you are his beloved child, his friend, who he delights to spend time with. His deepest desire is to see you whole, healed, at peace, restored.

As you rest in him, it brings him glory. The rest *is* worship.

We've printed the Message version of Matthew 11:28-30 on the next page. Sit with it, receiving this invitation from Jesus. Allow yourself to relax into the welcome of God. Know the lightness of his company. Receive his rest.

Are you tired?

Worn out?

Burned out on religion?

Come to me.

Get away with me and you'll
recover your life.

I'll show you how to take a real rest.

Walk with me and work with me
- watch how I do it.

Learn the unforced
rhythms of grace.

I won't lay anything heavy or
ill-fitting on you.

Keep company with me and you'll
learn to live freely and lightly.